FINDING AND PREPARING PRECIOUS AND SEMIPRECIOUS STONES

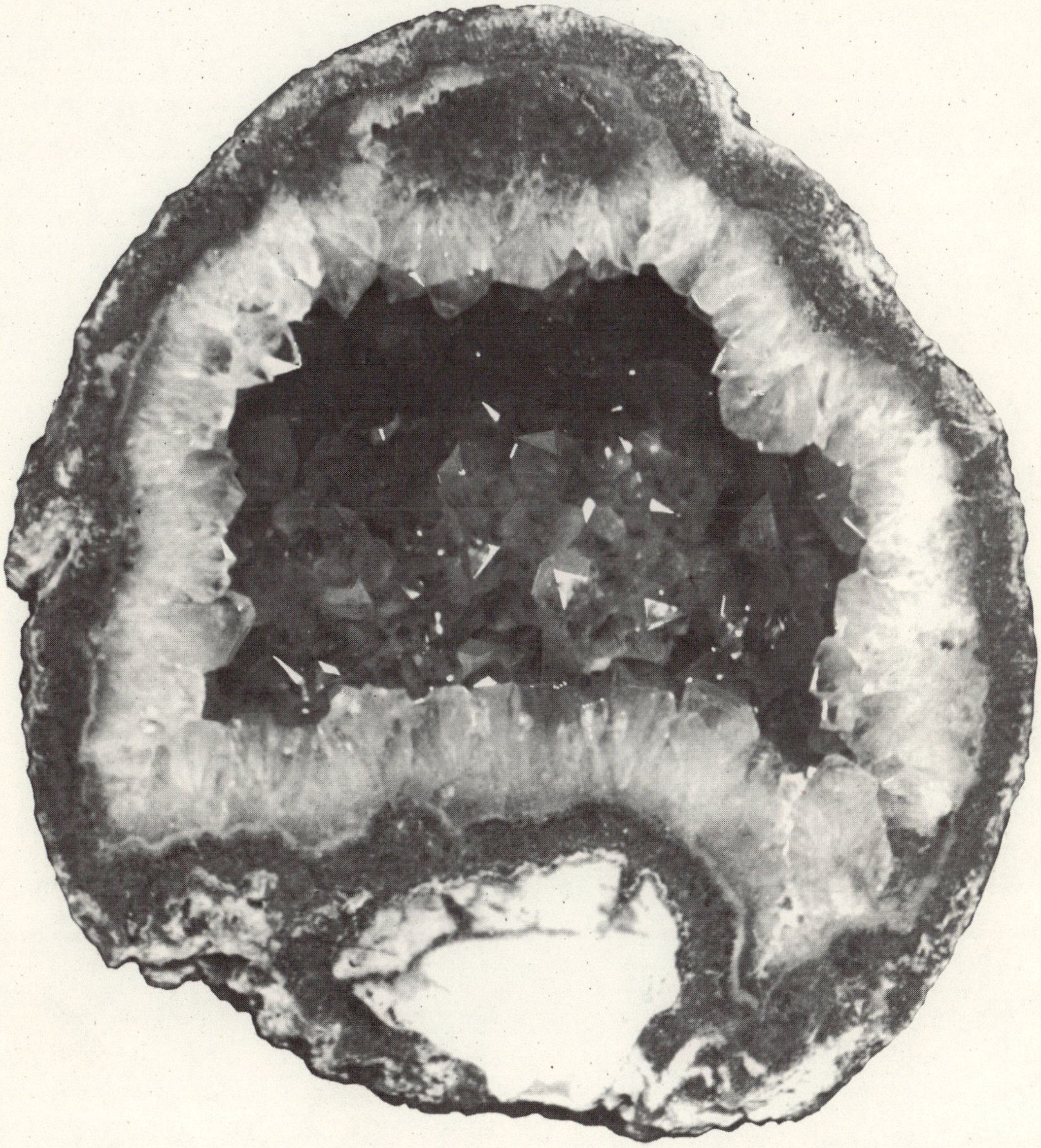

Other hobby books in this series include:

Jewelry Making as a Hobby
Clock Repairing as a Hobby
Watch Repairing as a Hobby

FINDING AND PREPARING PRECIOUS AND SEMIPRECIOUS STONES

JAMES A. PETERSON

Photographs by Mike Caggiano

ASSOCIATION PRESS • New York

FINDING AND PREPARING
PRECIOUS AND SEMIPRECIOUS STONES

Association Press, 291 Broadway, New York, N.Y. 10007

International Standard Book Number: 0-8096-1826-5
Library of Congress Catalog Card Number: 74-1276

The pictures of gold-in-quartz, smithsonite, stilbite, and wulfenite on the front cover and the picture of the amethyst geode on page 1 are reproduced by courtesy of John Grieger of Grieger's, Inc., from specimens in his personal collection.

Library of Congress Cataloging in Publication Data

Peterson, James Alfred.
Finding and preparing precious and semiprecious stones.

Bibliography: p.94.
1. Precious stones—Collectors and collecting—United States. I. Title.
QE392.5.U5P47 553'.8'075 74-1276

ISBN 0-8096-1826-5

PRINTED IN THE UNITED STATES OF AMERICA

Contents

Preface

SOME TEN MILLION men and women in the United States pursue the little known trails and lanes of the country in a continuing effort to discover precious and semi-precious stones. In many cases, they work harder at their hobby than they do in earning money to make such trips possible. They sacrifice comfort and time to hold in their hands a single specimen of a gemstone never before seen by human eyes. Then they round it and polish it and set it with such expertise that its glory is enhanced. They could probably buy a similar specimen in a rock shop or jewelry store for a fraction of what their trip cost in the way of both money and energy. But to a rockhound his discovery and his own fabrication gives him a creative satisfaction that few other experiences in life can equal. Some of these rockhounds achieve great expertise and share their skill in the journals of lapidary communication; others simply enjoy the quest and the discovery. This book shares with you some pointers about the search for, and about the preparation of, these specimens.

J.A.P.

1. In the Beginning

THE BEGINNING ROCKHOUND must know something about rocks, just as a physician who specializes in ear, nose and throat must necessarily know a great deal about the total body. If a rockhound does not know the relationship of crystals to various kinds of rock formation he may spend his life searching for particular gems in the wrong places. Many of the great uranium discoveries resulted from the prospector's awareness that uranium is radioactive and thus can be detected by the aid of special electrical detectors. The collector will have as much success as he has knowledge about the rock world.

Furthermore, in the beginning the world was rock and it is still rock. There is nothing of permanent substance on this earth that is not rock. To learn something about the history of and changes in the rocks that make up our environment is to become acquainted with the basic building blocks of our world. The science of geology can be described as classification of rocks and the processes which characterize their change. Most of the great mineral and gem discoveries of the world have been made by men who knew rocks, their characteristics and their relationships with minerals. This chapter describes in simple terms the composition of the crust of our earth. The following charts present in schematic form the relationship of chemical elements, rocks and minerals.

The earth's crust is formed from indivisible chemical elements such as oxygen, silicon, aluminum, iron, calcium, sodium, potassium and magnesium. These eight are mentioned because they are the most important and in different combinations make up most of the igneous rocks on earth. It is the different combinations of the elements which create the differences in color, sheen, hardness, etc., which we shall mention later. Two of these elements, aluminum and oxygen, when combined in the particular proportion of two parts aluminum and three parts oxygen form the minerals ruby and sapphire. The pigeon-blood red of the ruby is thought to result from traces of chromic oxide and the blues and greens of the sapphire from traces of titanium oxide.

Three great classes of rock make up the face of the earth. Igneous rocks are the original rocks that were formed when the earth's surface first cooled and solidified. During the first few millions of years of earth there were no other types. However, as the waves and the rain and the wind attacked those rocks they crumbled and were swept into the sea. There these sediments combined with the bones of early sea creatures and all these formed a deep deposit on the floor of the sea. The enormous weight and pressure of the water pressed them together until they formed a hard, solid mass, thus creating a second great class of rocks called Sedimentary rocks. As the crust of the earth continued to cool and contract, it was subjected to breaking, bending and squeez-

Chart I

BASIC RELATIONSHIPS BETWEEN ELEMENTS, MINERALS AND ROCKS

Basic Elements (102)

combine to form

↓

Minerals

combine to form

↓

Rocks

ing. The result was the transformation of the nature of the rock itself, the emergence of new chemicals and new formations. An example of the radical change that occurred is the change of limestone into marble. This third great type of rock is called Metamorphic rock.

Even as the 102 chemical elements can combine to form an almost infinite number of chemical compounds, so the chemicals can combine to form many different classes of igneous, sedimentary and metamorphic rocks. Here are several facts that will help you to differentiate among igneous rocks. Those rocks having relatively large proportions of iron and magnesium (technically ferromagnesian minerals) are dark and those without are light. The practical application of this comes when one learns that such minerals as mica, apatite, sphene, zircon, fluroite and corundum are associated with light-colored igneous rocks and magnetite, ilmenite, pyrite and pyrrhotite are associated with dark igneous rocks. The minerals associated with igneous rocks are differentiated also in terms of the length of cooling time that went on in volcanic or other processes. The obsidians are minerals that had no time to grow large crystals because they cooled almost immediately, and their smooth, glasslike texture is easily identified.

We have described the formation of sedimentary rocks as resulting from the decomposition of igneous rocks. Anyone who walks in the mountains will be familiar with the natural processes going on there. Vegetation is abundant, with roots making cracks which later admit water which freezes. The harsh wind carries sand which scrapes the rock, and rain washes it down. Glaciers not only cut huge valleys but they also grind the rock into such small pieces that sometimes it resembles flour and thus becomes clay. Changes in temperature expand and contract the rock until large cracks and fissures appear. As they wash down to the river beds and sea, the minerals that are the heaviest sink to the bottom and often are arrested there. At the Eldorado sapphire mine in Montana the action of a million years is readily apparent. The river deposited the minerals

Chart II

SPECIFIC ILLUSTRATION OF RELATIONSHIPS BETWEEN ELEMENTS, MINERALS AND ROCKS

Elements involved ——————→ $AL_2 0_3$
which combine to form

Minerals ——————→ Rubies and Sapphires (Corundum)
which combine with Biotite Mica to form

Rock ——————→ Igneous Dike Rock

on the bedrock. Layer after layer was accumulated; some layers are rich with gold and sapphires and others have none, depending on the source of the sediments. Often the layer lying directly on the bedrock has changed from gravel and is now an almost concrete-like hard rock while above it is gravel. One of the most rewarding of the sedimentary deposits is the placer where gold, gems and other minerals are deposited. The most abundant minerals in placers are rubies and sapphires, diamonds, spinel and zircon.

The rockhound will soon learn that gravel beds are rich in such minerals as quartz, feldspar, mica, garnet, tourmaline, magnetite, zircon, gold, platinum, topaz, beryl, ruby and sapphire. One important rock in this group is limestone because it is often the final resting place of fossils such as shellfish, corals, crinoids and algae. Limestone weathers relatively quickly and to this we owe some of the most striking natural sculpture.

While not particularly attractive as a collector's item, the formation of coal is interesting. It has very little mineral substance but has been formed by pressure on vegetable matter. All through the middle Northwest one can see bands of almost black substance between layers of sedimentary rock. This is coal formed in a very unique way. Ferns, tree leaves and many other vegetable forms may be identified in layers of this lignite, or soft coal. Hard coal, which is much less porous, has none of these remains. There have been some discoveries of amber associated with lignite coal in Eastern America, but not in the West. Amber is defined as a fossil resin of coniferous trees. It is yellow to yellowish-brown.

Metamorphic rocks were described as those which resulted from chemical or environmental changes. Gneiss is a granitelike rock that forms many different kinds of rock. A gneiss rock looks something like granite with bands of coloration. The schist are similar to the gneiss but have a greater tendency to decomposition. They are associated with more interesting minerals than are the gneiss rocks. Schists often contain feldspar, garnet, mica and quartz.

With sapphires are often found associated an abundance of hematite. Hematite was formed from original sedimentary deposits of iron carbonate and iron silicate which, when subjected to intense heat and pressure, became iron oxide, or hematite. Water plays an important part in this process and hematite is often found in the form of an ancient animal form which was filled in by the iron oxide. Chalcedony, one of the common varieties of quartz, was formed in the same way.

Pegmatites and Hematites

As the earth's surface contracted, buckled and cracked it left apertures. These often went very deep into the earth's surface and provided escape channels for liquids and gases which were under great pressure below the crust. That liquid contained a mixture of rare minerals, silicates, and extremely hot water. Sometimes only gas and vapor escaped. The escaping liquids and gases tended over the centuries to concentrate the minerals in the fissures. Where the material deposited contains as its principal components feldspar, quartz and mica it is known as pegmatite. Most of our metals and gems come from the liquids that were brought to the surface in this way.

If the fissure is a crack that is perpendicular to the surface it is called a dike. If it is horizontal it is called a sill, and if it is round it is called a pipe. These cavities occur in a great variety of shapes and range in length from a foot to several thousands of feet. A good example of a dike is the Yogo Gulch in central Montana. This dike extends for several miles. It varies from ten to fifty feet in width. The dike intrudes a sloping bed of limestone. As the Yogo mine has been worked at various times in the past hundred years, the material in the dike has been removed so that it is possible to see the sharp differences between the rock that forms the dike and the surrounding walls.

Hematites in the perfect form of an early sea animal are often found. This process by which the original organic matter is supplanted by silica is known as *replacement.* Large ore deposits are often replacements of original minerals by new minerals. A further process is the simple one of weathering in which original rocks are destroyed and minerals are released to combine with other minerals to form new compounds. It is thought that turquoise was produced by this process. In a sense this is the opposite of the pegmatite formation because here rain water carries decomposed elements down into the seams, while with pegmatites the elements were carried up into the cavities from the liquids below.

In addition to the importance of identifying dikes, sills and pipes it is important for the rockhound to think about the ways in which time has modified the appearance and the structure of mineral-bearing deposits. On many mountains the pegmatites have been covered with vegetation and eroded material. Some detective work is often necessary in order to discover these rich bearing pegmatites. Furthermore, once they have been discovered it is important to determine their extent. The ability to locate placers is a highly rewarding art indeed, for there are to be found the concentrations of minerals and gems that the collector desires. Sometimes the talus slopes at the base of a mountain contain rich indications of a dike or sill above. These should always be examined for some clue as to what has been washed and blown down from a higher elevation. There is a talus slope in the Antelope Valley in Southern California where the rock fragments seemed to have a rich, deep and heavy appearance. Closer inspection revealed that these rocks had a very deceptive volcanic surface. They were really agates with rather magnificent palm-root inclusions. They were scattered in such richness that one could gather enough good material without even looking for their source. Again, some of the best specimens from Emerald Creek in Idaho have been found by individuals standing in the middle of the stream and digging down five or six feet where the garnets had accumulated over the centuries. On the other hand, just as good material came from the side of the banks several feet above the water. It was perfectly obvious that the garnets had washed into the river valley from the hills about, and that the flatland or present banks of the stream had also once been washed by the stream. Figure 1 illustrates some of the areas that have been described as promising for prospecting.

Crystals

The great mass of solid matter is made up of crystals, which were formed when the mineral matter in liquid or gaseous form became solid. Crystals are generally regarded as being among the most perfect forms in nature. Innumerable molecules are stacked in perfect order and alignment. It is estimated that it would be rare to find even one atom out of a thousand not in place. Yet some of the subtle and lovely colors that make crystals attractive to us for gem collecting purposes are due to such minute imperfections.

Crystals are said to have faces or sides. It is rare to find a perfect gem because as the gem has been tumbled over and over and knocked against other rocks it often has lost its distinctive shape. Sometimes the abrasive contact with other hard rocks has rounded it off until all its sides are also gone. Crystals occur in all sizes from microscopic to enormous masses several feet in dimension. One of the most famous was the single beryl stone found in Oxford County in Maine that weighed 18 tons and was 18 feet in length.

Few subjects have been studied and analyzed so completely as has crystallography in the past two decades. The crystals formed by each mineral are distinctive because each molecule determining that mineral is attracted and repulsed in an invariable pattern. Thus the shape, the angles and the general form of mineral crystals are always the same for a given classification. Some minerals develop in a "twinning" manner, which means that the total crystal looks as though it were composed of two similar shapes back to back. Another phenomenon is "grouping" in which a large number of crystals grow together in parallel formation. In this case the axes of all the crystals are parallel. A much-sought-after form of chalcedony, gypsum and hematite is called rosette because it resembles the rose.

Among the more favored collection items for many rockhounds are minerals with "inclusions." This means that a transparent crystal contains another mineral or other matter within its form. Quartz is well known for this phenomenon, often containing

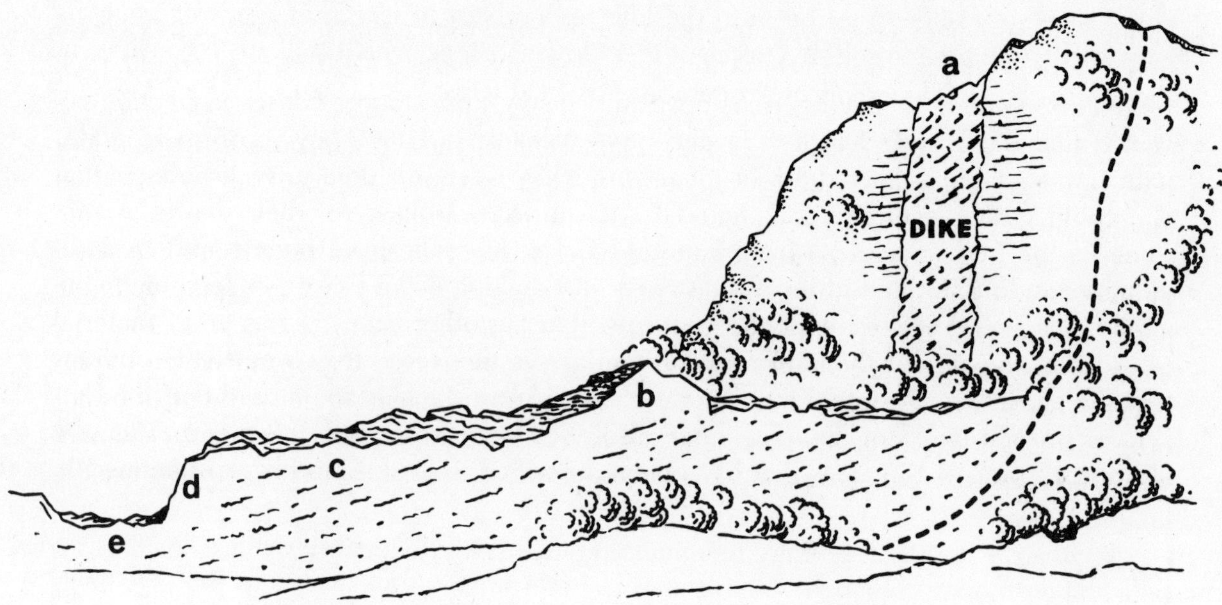

FIGURE 1. PROSPECTING LOCATIONS OF INTEREST

a. This represents the original dike which contributed the minerals represented in this area. However, the dotted line represents a possible situation in which weathering has now obliterated the dike and all minerals are gone from the original place.

b. This represents the talus pile where diligent search may discover minerals both on the surface and below.

c. This flat valley area possibly represents the old stream bed and may be rich in deposits. Almost all dredging has been done on areas like this.

d. This represents the present walls of the stream and must be carefully mined because the concentration of minerals may in fact be richer here than in the bed of the stream.

e. If it is possible to mine the bed of the stream itself this may prove to be rich in deposits. Many present-day gold miners are using pumps to explore this possibility.

such other minerals as hematite, garnet, tourmaline, gold, etc. Inclusions in diamonds, emeralds, garnets or sapphires detract from their value. On the other hand, inclusions in agate give the characteristic effect that makes moss agate so valuable. An example is the moss agate of eastern Montana which sometimes produces scenes of unbelievable verisimilitude to a sunset, a pine tree, or an abstract painting.

Most mineral and gem collectors are actually collecting crystals, and thus an extensive knowledge of crystal growth adds a great deal of pleasure to the pursuit. An awareness of original crystal forms gives the gem collector a basis on which to judge the accuracy of his identification as well as to visualize the original state of the specimen.

This chapter has given only the most simple introduction to the origin of rocks and minerals, and to crystallography. In the beginning it is more important to whet the appetite than to saturate it. Anyone who is going to immerse himself in rockhounding will want to study each of these aspects of background information in detail. The hobbyist who wishes to go out into the hills and valleys in search of gems or minerals may well prepare himself by taking the following steps which will be rewarding in themselves as well as excellent preparation for field trips:

1. Join a mineral society or a rock club. Both of these organizations provide lectures on basic geology and crystallography. Furthermore, the general conversation among the people who join such clubs is educational in itself.

2. Take a geology or mineralogy course. A great many adult-education curriculums in our cities now give quite adequate courses in geology and mineralogy. These courses generally involve field trips under the supervision of an expert so that the knowledge gained is not simply from lecture. It pays to take courses in which the instructor leads his classes out into the field. If the adult-education department does not offer such courses, look up the curriculum in a community college or in an evening school of a nearby college or university. The cost is minimal, but the course is usually taught by experts.

3. Read a standard geology or mineralogy textbook; select one with color illustrations. Then mount your own exhibit of rocks and minerals according to the classifications given in the textbook. There is nothing that equals this experience in beginning to differentiate the basic types of rock or to become familiar with pegmatite formations.

4. Visit repeatedly one of the nearest permanent mineral and gem exhibits in your locality. There are excellent museums with this type of exhibit in every part of the country. Study the exhibits in relation to the classifications you are learning from the textbook.

5. Attend mineral and gem shows. These do not have the comprehensive nature of permanent collections, but many of them offer ample opportunity for study. Most specimens are labeled. If they are not labeled and you are perplexed, ask the exhibitor to tell you about the specimen. You will thus learn a good deal both about the mineral and the locality where it was discovered.

6. Read specialized books dealing with this subject.

This chapter has told something about the complexity of rock formations, how minerals were formed and where they are located. This information is the ground on which later expositions will be built concerning gemstones themselves and where they are discovered. Fortunately many have visited the field before us and we can profit by their experiences. But before we talk about field trips we need to know what we are looking for. This will concern us in the next chapter.

2. What Gems Do You Hunt?

WHAT DOES THE rockhound hunt? The answer is, of course, that he hunts gems. The next question follows naturally. How does he recognize them? This chapter is devoted to two major expositions of that subject. We will consider the ways in which we identify gems and then we will discuss the gems themselves. One cannot describe gems, however, until one knows something about gem characteristics. Our discussion will begin with these characteristics. Then we will describe the gemstones themselves.

Identification Rules

All gems possess certain basic characteristics in common, such as color, degree of hardness, cleavage propensities, sheen and chemical composition. Within this overall framework, however, each class of gems also differ among themselves in the degree to which they possess each of these characteristics, so that there are several ways of making positive identification. One common way to identify gems is by using some test to determine their relative hardness.

Hardness. We know that stones vary in their permeability or hardness. Chalk rubs off on anything (unfortunately for college professors' clothing), but a diamond or sapphire leaves no trace on contact. An ingenious attempt to discriminate scientifically between gems was made by an early scientist, Frederick Mohs. He developed a scale of hardness into which all gems fall. It is not a true scale because the degree of hardness between the classes is not equal as the distance between inches is equal on a foot rule. Nevertheless, his scale is accurate enough for the practical needs of the gem collector. It is very useful. The scale moves from 1 through 10 and is identified with one gem for each classification:

The Mohs Scale

1. Talc (softest)	6. Feldspar
2. Gypsum	7. Quartz
3. Calcite	8. Topaz
4. Fluorite	9. Corundum
5. Apatite	10. Diamond (hardest)

This is a very old scale and in some ways it is difficult to follow. In most of the cases each point on the scale is indicated by a distinctive stone like a diamond or a topaz. On the other hand corundum is a more general classification. Rubies and sapphire are corundum stones. Despite these difficulties, however, this scale is the one that is universally used and it will be helpful to us as we describe the individual characteristics of various precious and semiprecious stones. On this Mohs scale any mineral can scratch or mark all those listed above it and in turn it can be scratched by those below it. Rockhounds have learned that many common objects can be used to test the hardness of a find. Thus a fingernail will scratch talc and gypsum, a copper coin will mark calcite. A knife blade will make a mark on fluorite and apatite, and a topaz will scratch feldspar and quartz. Only corundum and diamond will mark topaz, but corundum will not scratch a diamond. Suppose one found a piece of very clear (noncolored) material that seemed very hard but which had been tumbled and worn through the centuries so that it had no distinctive shape. It might be quartz, topaz, corundum or diamond. Unless one had some way of distinguishing what it was it would remain an unknown. However, by means of the hardness test one could assign it to its proper category. If the rockhound carried with him the common items mentioned above plus a piece of topaz or sapphire (which is corundum) he could make the identification. Many rockhounds do, in fact, carry the items mentioned above. There is a certain value in developing expertise in identification, but practice is required in using hardness tests.

Crystal Forms. If one is fortunate enough to find crystals in their original forms they tend to be unique in appearance so that familiarity with the forms helps in identification. The sapphire has a six-sided form. Often a typical V-shaped thin termination may still be seen on either end. Its length is greater than its circumference. An emerald, on the other hand, while six-sided, has a regular barlike shape with a flat termination on both ends. A garnet is eight-sided, but may have many shapes. Fluorite is a cube, and hematite often is found in perfect cubes. The novice rockhound can soon learn these distinctive shapes by visiting mineral shows and museums. Of course there are some shapes, such as that of the cross-shaped staurolite, that are so distinctive that once viewed they are not readily forgotten.

There are many other shapes which the gem collector should come to recognize with no difficulty. A ball- or sphere-shaped heavy stone should always be studied because its irregular and pitted surface may often hide a geode that may have beautiful

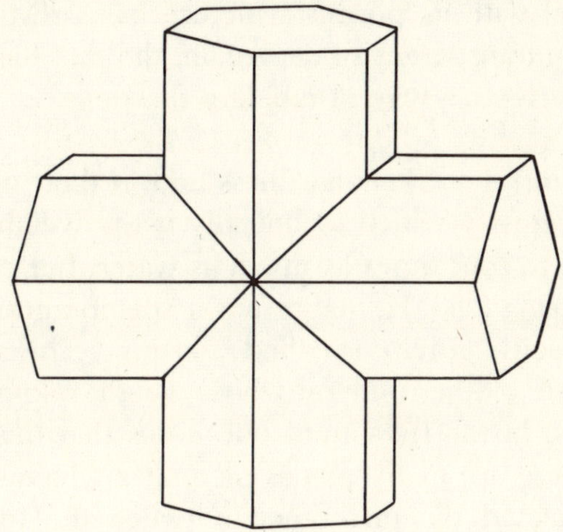

FIGURE 2. TWINNED CRYSTAL OF STAUROLITE

crystals inside. Sometimes the surface of a geode is knobby and sometimes smooth. But the shape is definitive. Incidentally, the harder the stone, the sharper the angles.

Luster. Every mineral reflects light in a different way from others. This is because of its differing chemical composition and its hardness. In Wyoming one may find a group of stones all lying in a small cluster that look a bit shiny, much as though they had been coated by a light oil. These are gizzard stones (gastroliths), or stones the dinosaur used in his gizzard for grinding up his food. Closely related to an oily look is that of a silky appearance such as satin spar. Other gems, such as topaz and some Montana agates, appear to have been sandblasted; their surface is finely pitted and presents an opaque appearance. Jasper of a fine grade has many colors but is translucent. It seems to absorb light, but is not clear enough to see through. Quartz, sapphire, fine emerald, some agate, some obsidian, topaz and diamonds are glassy or have a vitreous luster.

Cleavage. Cleavage means exactly what the word implies . . . where the stone tends to split apart. If one takes mica as an illustration, its cleavage characteristics are all too apparent because it has a "tablet" appearance and comes apart between layers. Most gems break in consistent ways along smooth surfaces. Some gems are said not to cleave but to *fracture* because they behave like glass.

Color. One would think that color would be of inestimable help in identifying minerals and gems, but it is only useful in certain limited ways. It is also a difficult part of the identification procedure because so many gems come in the same colors. There are blue sapphires, blue diamonds, blue topza, blue azurite, blue quartz; so that, in general, color does not aid in distinguishing between gems. On the other hand, there are special gems whose color is so distinctive that it serves as an excellent clue. A case in point is amethyst. This gem has a distinctive purplish or bluish-violet color that once noted can hardly be forgotten. Jade comes in various shades of green, but its fibrous quality and its toughness make it a unique stone. Turquoise is blue, blue-green and green; but, again, this opaque mineral with its porous structure has a distinctive look. Opal in its most elegant form is a semitransparent stone. Again, the fact that the color presentation is unique makes color an effective way of labeling this gem.

Specific Gravity. Gems differ in their hardness and in their weight. The weight of a gem is called its specific gravity which technically is the weight of water it displaces. Garnet weighs from three to four times as much as water, but an emerald weighs much less, its specific gravity being 2.63. Hematite has a specific gravity of five. A very useful and simple test for specific gravity is called "hefting." This simply means lifting the gem and comparing it with another mineral whose weight is known. This test may seem fuzzy, but one is not long in the field until one notes that this test is used by almost everyone. At our mine there are many pieces of quartz which screen out with the sapphires. Most persons detected the difference between the two by using luster and hefting as their means of detection.

If one wants a far more precise way of using specific gravity to differentiate stones he may purchase or build a scale which weighs the stone in water. The formula is:

$$\text{Specific gravity} = \frac{\text{weight in air}}{\text{weight in air} - \text{weight in water}}$$

There are several well-known scales of this type; the Rogers and the Jolly balance scales are simple but accurate measures.

Out in the field you may often notice a rockhound take out a pocket magnifier or use an eye loupe to look at a stone. This rockhound is studying the growth lines (successive deposits over a period of time), capillary tubes, gas liquid or mineral inclusion and minute cracks, which help him identify the stone and determine its value. This method of detection is invaluable in differentiating synthetic from natural corundum stones. On the basis of these characteristics we can now form something of a catalogue of precious and semiprecious stones. This will tell us *which* specific gems we wish to hunt. *Where* to find them will be discussed in the next chapter.

Precious Gems

Diamonds. The diamond is the gem of gems. It is unparalleled in its hardness, brilliance, fire and rarity. It is found only by rare chance in the United States outside of one area near Murfreesboro, Arkansas, where there is a crater in which tourists are allowed to search for diamonds. The Arkansas area is genuine volcanic kimberlite. This means that it resembles rather exactly the round spoutlike formation in which diamonds are found throughout the world.

Some diamonds have been found in the Midwest, where they were evidently deposited by the great glacial "ice plows"; other diamonds have been found scattered in stream beds on the west slopes of the Sierra Nevada in California and a few scattered stones have been located at other sites. The possibility of finding a diamond in any of these areas is so slight, however, that to recommend hunting them is to invite frustration and disappointment. And, as a result, most rockhounds acquire their diamonds by purchase or trade. Many collectors prefer a collection of colored diamonds or those that were faceted many years ago which exhibit some of the earlier cutting designs. They are often used in combination with other gems by way of contrast.

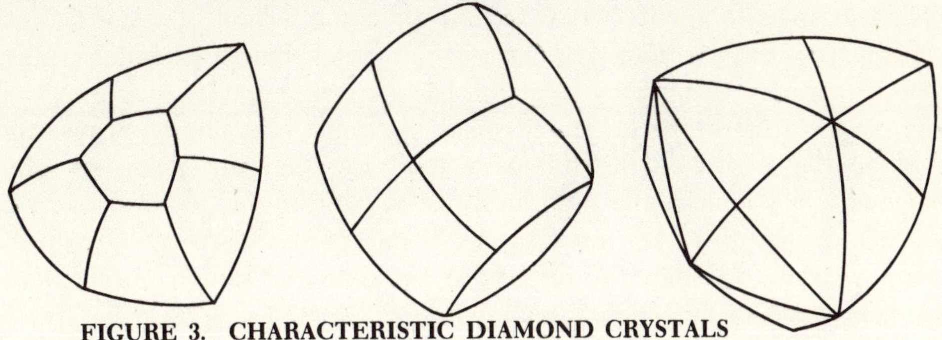

FIGURE 3. CHARACTERISTIC DIAMOND CRYSTALS

The diamond has certain distinctive characteristics. It is the hardest gem discovered and so is at the top of the Mohs scale with a 10 rating. It can be scratched only by another diamond. Its pure crystal form is cubic or octahedron. Its cleavage characteristic is parallel to the faces on the crystal. Its specific gravity ranges from 3.516 to 3.525. In its original crystal form the diamond has a brilliant but somewhat greasy luster. A diamond crystal that is not marred by fractures or any inclusions and that is faceted correctly shows brilliant color flashes unique among all the clear gemstones.

Sapphires and Rubies. These two gems are grouped because, with the single exception of color, they have the same characteristics. Rubies are red, while sapphires come in many colors. Sapphires are the most abundant precious stones in the United States. These gems are found with asterism, with stars, and in clear states. Asterism is caused by fibrous inclusions and many such stones can be cut so that they have a "sun" on the crown. Star sapphires and rubies occur when the fibrous inclusions are arranged in groups about 60 degrees apart. The clear stones are cherished if they have deep color. Many clear stones, however, show an unevenness of color. If the faceter concentrates a rich golden or blue spot at the point of the culot (the base point of the faceted stone) that color permeates the entire stone. Schlegel states that the "finest gems are cut from large, perfect stones with even color," but the author disagrees. A skilled alignment of the stone often produces an unusual gem even if the color is uneven. Of course the larger the stone the more valuable the gem.

Sapphires and rubies are found in North Carolina, Colorado, Idaho, Indiana, California and Montana, but they appear only in any great volume in gem quality in Montana. Specific localities for each gem will be given later. The characteristics of sapphires and rubies are as follows: They are very hard but not as hard as a diamond. They rate 9 on the Mohs scale. They can be scratched only by a diamond or by another corundum stone. Their crystal form is a hexagonal rod. In their original crystal form there is a very thinly formed V or triangle on the bottom or top of the crystal. Corundum is the heaviest of all gem material with a specific gravity of 3.95 to 4.10. Thus a carat of sapphire is somewhat smaller than a carat of diamond. Sapphires and rubies usually have a glassy look, but if they have been well worn by tossing in a stream they will look somewhat sanded. Corundum has a rather simple chemical composition, being formed of two parts aluminum and three parts oxygen with minute traces of other chemicals that make for

**FIGURE 4.
SAPPHIRE WITH TERMINATION**

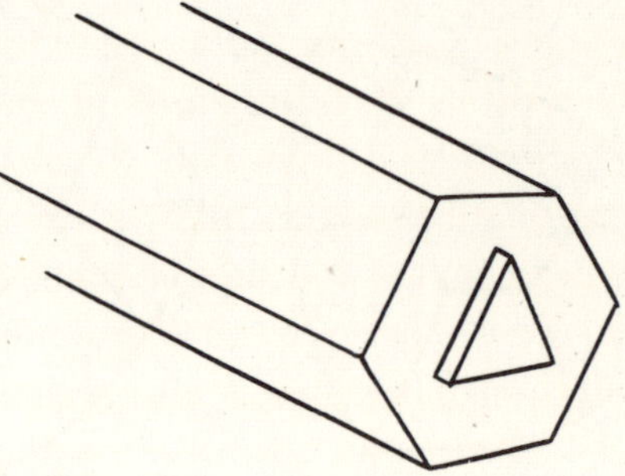

the different colors. Rubies are pigeon blood red, while sapphires come in many colors, such as pink, purple or green.

Emerald. The emerald is regarded by Schlegel as the only precious form of beryl. This may be debated because many collectors also prize a fine piece of aquamarine as a very distinctive gem. The emerald may be vitreous (resembling glass), but in less perfect gems somewhat clouded. Emeralds have been found in a few places in the United States (Maine, Massachusetts, Nevada, North Carolina among them), but production in this country does not compare in quality or quantity with the imported stones. The rock-hunter would do well to concentrate on hunting other varieties of beryl which are to be found in greater abundance in this country. The quality of the emerald is determined by its color and degree of transparency. Many emeralds of lesser quality are almost opaque because of their cloudiness.

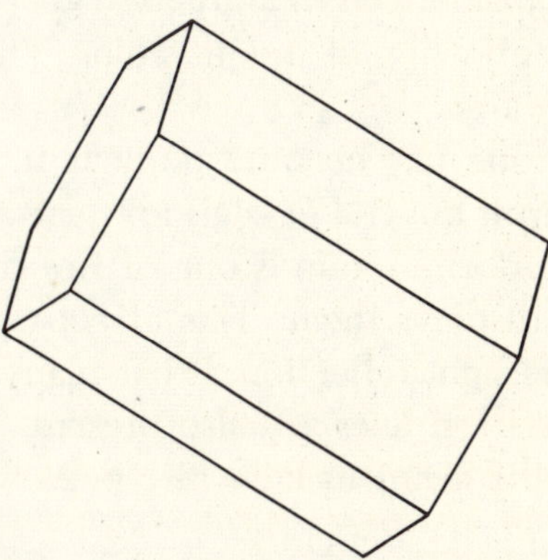

FIGURE 5. TYPICAL EMERALD CRYSTAL

The characteristics of the emerald are as follows: It has a medium hardness of 7.5 on the Mohs scale. Thus the emerald can be scratched by a diamond, ruby, sapphire, or topaz. It has a hexagonal crystal form with flat terminations. It is only half as heavy as corundum stones, with a specific gravity of from 2.63 to 2.80. Thus a one-carat emerald is almost twice as large as a one-carat sapphire. In its original form it has a glassy or a clouded luster. It is always grass-green in color. Chemically it is composed of beryllium, aluminum, silicon and oxygen.

Semiprecious Gems

Beryl. Varieties of beryl that are regarded as less precious than emerald are aquamarine, heliodor and morganite. As with rubies and sapphires, these stones share the same characteristics with the emerald, but they differ in color. The aquamarine is bluish green, the heliodor is golden yellow, and morganite is red or pink. Aquamarine is found in greater frequency and in many more locations than the yellow and red stones. Beryl occurs in California, Colorado, Connecticut, Georgia, Idaho, Maine, Maryland, New Hampshire, New York, North Carolina, Pennsylvania, South Carolina, South Dakota and Utah. Other than color, characteristics of aquamarine, heliodor and morganite are the same as those of emerald discussed above.

Feldspar. Many rockhounds regard the groups of gems belonging to this classification as being somewhat mysterious. No specimen may be found in their immediate locality and so the names of the gems may seem esoteric. They do form a strange group if one considers only nomenclature. Who would believe that the moonstone and sunstone were made of the same elements? Not to mention amazonite, labradorite and oligoclase, in which the root word is a combination of geographical name and chemical terminology? As a rule, in the past gems were named fortuitously and not logically. Still these stones are not only uniquely lovely but they are quite abundant in many places. If the gem collector dismisses them offhand, he will have sacrificed much beauty from his collection. For instance, moonstone, although predominantly white often has a somewhat opalescent bluish tone that makes it unique.

Amazonite is a gem widely dispersed throughout the United States. Its color ranges from a bluish-green to a greenish gray. It is more opaque than is moonstone, but can be cut as a cabochon of unique color. The Pikes Peak area in Colorado is the best-known collecting area.

Sunstone has become popular in the last ten years. It has an unique appearance because iron mineral crystals are scattered throughout this gem. It "cabs" well.

Labradorite reminds one of fire opal that has become gentle. Rather than flashing colors it displays them. This effect comes from the reflection of several minerals that distort the light reflection. It has many colors, predominantly blue and gray, but green, yellow and red hues are also present. This gem has been located chiefly in the Adirondacks, but specimens have also been found in Arkansas, New Mexico, Texas, Utah and Vermont.

Oligoclase presents itself in clear, vitreous crystals and is therefore much prized. It is also rare. Schlegel has no reference to any location of this gem in the United States, but McFall suggests that "transparent feldspar" can be found in Maine and Utah. We assume he is speaking of oligoclase.

6. AMAZONITE CRYSTAL

The characteristics of feldspar are these: It is much softer than any of the gems discussed so far, with a location on the Mohs scale of 6.0 to 6.5. This means that it can be scratched by garnet, topaz, corundum or the diamond. The feldspars are very light, with a specific gravity of 2.45 to 2.75. This means that a feldspar gem of one carat would be about the same size as that of an emerald gem. The color varies as described previously. In general the chemicals that combine to form the feldspars are potassium, aluminum, silicate and oxygen. Variations in the distributions of these chemicals account for the different types of feldspar.

Garnets. Garnets are a ubiquitous and intriguing group of stones. It is not an exaggeration to say that they occur almost everywhere. Half the states have one or several varieties of this gem. However, the gems vary widely in color and in value, so that the collector must have at least a rudimentary background of knowledge about gems in order to dig or buy garnets intelligently. Last year a neighbor of mine went to a church rummage sale; while there she found a necklace of "pretty, red stones." As it was marked to sell for twenty-five cents, she bought it. Later, while talking about it, she said: "I was not going to buy it if it was fifty cents." On my wife's advice she had the necklace appraised by her jeweler who put a conservative value of seventy-five dollars on her find. (It turned out that they were small, well-cut almandites, a form of garnet.) No doubt 98 per cent of the population would have reacted similarly. One of the satisfactions of the skilled rockhound is his ability to differentiate between types of gems in the same class. For example, there are six varieties of garnets. They vary in hardness, chemical composition, color and value. Most prized as gems are the fiery-red pyrope, the columbine-red almandite and the emerald-green andradite. Descriptions of the six classes follow:

1. *Almandite*
   The almandite is a "deep crimson, and violet or columbine red." It is relatively rare and is found in only five states. It is heavier than all other garnets with a

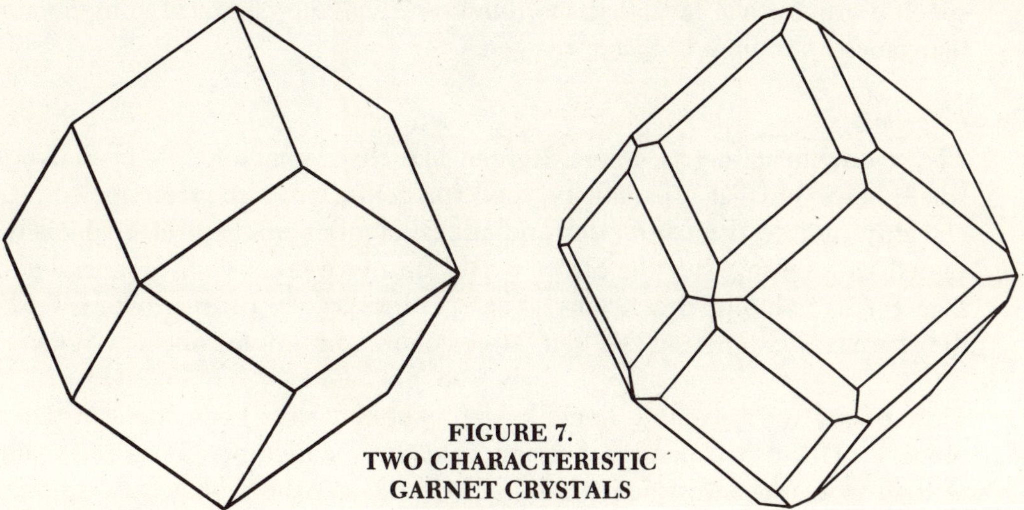

**FIGURE 7.
TWO CHARACTERISTIC
GARNET CRYSTALS**

specific gravity of 4.25. It is also very hard: 7.5 on the Mohs scale. Its chemical composition is iron, aluminum, silicon and oxygen.

2. *Andradite*
The andradite is a very common garnet and only two of its sub-varieties are used as gems; the emerald-green demantoid and the wine-yellow topazolite. These varieties are rare and have only been found in a few places in the eastern states. The andradite has a specific gravity of 3.75 and a hardness of 6.5 on the Mohs scale. It is made up of calcium, iron, silicon, oxygen.

3. *Grossularites*
The grossularite garnets are called cinnamon-stone, hyacinth or jacinth with characteristic color of golden-yellow or orange or reddish-brown. The colors are muddy and these stones are generally cloudy. The grossularite is not a favorite cutting stone, but a few are exceptional. The specific gravity is 3.53 and the hardness is 7.25. The stone is composed of calcium, aluminum, silicon, oxygen.

4. *Pyrope*
The pyrope garnet is very popular. In the United States it is associated with the Indians of Arizona and New Mexico, who have supplied much of the garnet material used by gem collectors in the last twenty-five years. Perhaps the best pyrope garnets are imported. When pyrope is combined with almandite it has a rose-red or purple cast and is called *rhodolite*. Its specific gravity is 3.51 and its hardness is 7.5. The chemical components are magnesium, aluminum, silicon and oxygen.

5. *Spessartite*
The Spessartite garnet is aurora red, yellow or orange brown. It is a rare find, but it is quite possible for the rockhound to trade for or buy a specimen. Its specific gravity is 4.18 and its hardness is 7.25. The chemical components are manganese, aluminum, silicon, oxygen.

6. *Uvarovite*
The uvarovite garnet is emerald green like the demantoid. Its crystals are so small, however, that it cannot be used for gems. It is also rare. One could conceivably tumble the *uvarovites* and use a number of them in a specially designed ring setting, but the effort would be more noteworthy for its ingenuity than for its value or practicality. The specific gravity of uvarovite is 3.52 and the chemicals composing this gem are calcium, chromium, silicon, oxygen.

Jade. Some of my most exciting hours as a rockhound have been spent in the spectacular scenery of British Columbia hunting jade. It is sometimes more rewarding to hunt jade than to work it, for jade is a tough, fibrous gemstone that is exasperatingly difficult to cut and finish. Nevertheless, when one perseveres jade has an uniqueness that intrigues almost every gem collector. This was demonstrated by the really overwhelming number of rockhounds who descended on the area of Lander, Wyoming, when significant jade discoveries were made there.

There are two kinds of jade and the ability to identify both of them is essential to the collector. Jadeite (emerald-green) is heavier and harder than the lesser-valued nephrite. The jade in Wyoming is nephrite. Some jadeite has been found in California. If the collector wants an experience of unsurpassed mountain scenery and wild life in addition to perhaps finding some excellent specimens, the author recommends a trip up the Fraser River in British Columbia. Truly remarkable specimens are becoming increasingly difficult to find, however, as the area has been expertly prospected.

The characteristics of jadeite and nephrite differ markedly, so they will be contrasted in this description. Both jadeite and nephrite have a medium hardness, but jadeite is slightly harder. Their respective hardnesses on the Mohs scale is 6.5 to 7.0 and 6.0 to 6.5. Again, jadeite is slightly heavier than nephrite, their specific gravity being 3.3 to 3.5 and 2.96 to 3.10 respectively. Both can be scratched with a steel file and by all of the gems with a hardness of 7 or more on the Mohs scale. The lustrous quality is unique and can be described as oily, cloudy and subvitreous. Both stones come in shades from white green to emerald green. Both have in common the chemical elements sodium, aluminum, silicon and oxygen, but nephrite also includes hydrogen, magnesium and iron. Just to indicate how complicated it may be to undertake a chemical analysis of gems the chemical formula for nephrite is given below. The small figures below each element indicate the proportion of each chemical that is combined with the others. The derivation of each chemical term in the equation is relatively simple with the exception of "Fe," which stands for iron. The chemical formula is:

$$Ca_2(Mg,Fe)_5\ (OH)_2\ (Si_4O_{11})2$$

Quartz. The quartz family is of great interest to the rockhound. Of course individual tastes differ but it is a safe guess that most collectors spend much of their time hunting and working with the various kinds of quartz. When one remembers that amethyst, along with the agates, chalcedonies, jaspers and the many varieties of quartz crystals are all associated with this group it is obvious that it is a very important classification. Furthermore, quartz is ubiquitous; it is everywhere and is available more readily than any other type of semiprecious gem. But more important are the startlingly beautiful varieties which intrigue everyone. Schlegel divides the quartz group into two subgroups: (*1*) the coarsely crystalline, and (*2*) the cryptocrystalline. The coarsely crystalline group can be cut into facets, but the second group is used mainly for cabochon presentations. Included in the coarsely crystalline classification are amethyst, tiger's-eye, citrine, milky quartz, quartz with inclusions such as prase and rutilated quartz, quartz crystal, rose quartz, and smoky quartz. The cryptocrystalline group includes all the varieties of agate, carnelian, chrysoprase, bloodstone, and jasper. A word of description follows to help identify each of these varieties:

Amethyst
The most valued type of quartz, amethyst varies in color from pale orchid to deep purple. It appears as a six-sided crystal often tapering toward the termination, which is pointed.

Tiger's-eye
Tiger's-eye is a quartz replacement of asbestos: the fibrous structure of the asbestos gives the intriguing chatoyant look. It is golden-brown.

Citrine
Citrine is a clear, yellow quartz much prized for its beauty. Because it looks so much like topaz, citrine has been called "false topaz."

Quartz with inclusions
This covers a wide variety of stones with mineral inclusions such as gold, hematite, rutile, tourmaline, etc.

Quartz crystal
Quartz crystal is the clear, colorless variety of quartz. The so-called "Herkimer diamond" is this type of small, clear quartz crystal named after the locality in New York where it is found.

Rose Quartz
Rose quartz is pale pink to deep rose in color.

Smoky Quartz
Smoky quartz is smoky-yellow to smoky brown in color. It is popular in gem cutting.

Agate
Agate has almost as many varieties as has quartz itself. Its most common colors are red, yellow, brown, green, blue, gray and black. It may be banded or homogeneous. It often has inclusions and then it is called "moss agate." If light brings out colors, it is called "iris agate." Thirty states contain one form or another of agate.

Carnelian
Carnelian is a clear stone ranging from yellow to red in color. It polishes well and has been used since early times for seals.

Chrysoprase
Chrysoprase is apple-green translucent quartz. Valued as a gem, the ancient Egyptians made it into beads.

Bloodstone
Bloodstone is a dark green, translucent quartz with red spots of jasper.

Jasper

Jasper comes in all colors, but generally in the same colors listed above for agate. It is, however, more opaque than agate or chalcedony. It is much prized for use in brooches, cuff links, and other jewelry. Every rock show has sections devoted to the unique pictures that can be isolated and mounted from this stone.

The characteristics of the quartz group are relatively consistent; and can be rather simply described: They have a medium hardness of 7 and can be scratched by garnet, topaz, corundum or diamond. They are quite light with a specific gravity of 2.58 to 2.66. Because they are relatively soft, light and inexpensive, it is recommended that initial experiments in cabochoning and faceting be made with stones from this group. They have a glassy and sometimes greasy luster. They vary in color. They have a very simple chemical composition, being composed of one part silicon and two parts oxygen; so it is very easy to write the chemical formula which describes them as: $Si0_2$.

Opal. The very best varieties of opal are regarded as precious but most opal is semiprecious. The opal is a semitransparent stone with red, yellow, green, blue or black colors. Its value comes from its fire, i.e., its ability to flash brilliant colors. This is called opalescence and the more vivid the display, the more valuable the stone. If opal is pure it is clear. The stone is so soft that it will break easily. Its chemical formula indicates that it contains water (H_20). Heat may cause that water to evaporate and shatter the stone. Opalized wood is a petrified wood in which the agent for change was an opaline chemical. Schlegel indicates that "very little precious opal has been found in the United States." Since her study, however, good fire opal has been located in at least ten states. The black opal that comes from the Virgin Valley in Nevada is of high quality, and two separate mines in Spencer, Idaho, are consistently producing precious opal.

The characteristics of opal are as follows: This stone is far down the scale of hardness, being measured at 5.5 to 6.5. It can be scratched by an iron file or by quartz. Thus, opal must be carefully treated when being cabochoned or while being worn as jewelry. It is also extremely light, with a specific gravity of only 1.0 to 2.3. Its luster is marked by waxy, resinous and subvitreous qualities. It appears in various color states or without color, being clear white or black, but in precious specimens always with flashing colors. It is not a complex stone in its chemical composition, as it is formed by only three elements: silicon, oxygen and hydrogen.

Topaz. Topaz is a transparent, glassy but not brilliant gem that comes in clear, pale brown, golden, blue and pinkish shades. It is prized for cutting as a gemstone because it has a hardness of 8 and some of its colors are beautiful. The wine-yellow or golden topaz is very distinctive. Some topaz tends to fade when subjected to sunlight. This seems to be particularly true of blue topaz. The collector should inquire about color permanence when collecting or buying this stone. It is found in ten states. Once the locality is specified, it is not hard to come by.

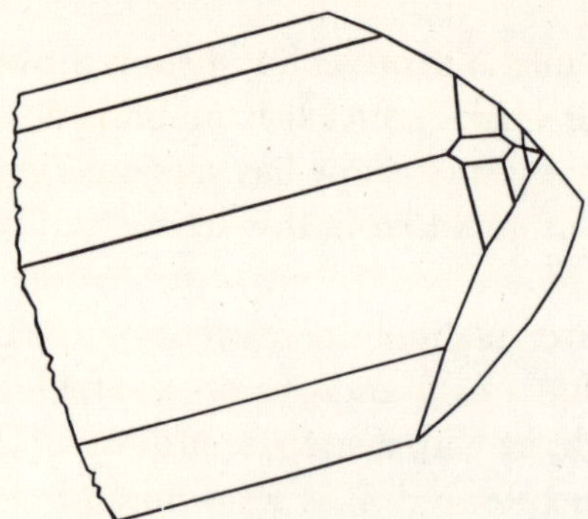

FIGURE 8. TOPAZ CRYSTAL

Tourmaline. Tourmaline is one of the most intriguing as well as being one of the most beautiful gems. It combines strongly contrasting colors that run perpendicular to the length of the thin crystal. There are the three types of alkali, magnesium and iron tourmaline. For those with a chemical bent it should be added that tourmaline is an aluminum silicate, but no amateur should try to analyze its components because its formula is extraordinarily complex. It has a very wide range of colors, exhibiting practically every known shade and tint with the exception of deep blue and emerald green. A popular stone is the so-called "watermelon tourmaline" which has a pink core and green exterior. One of the interesting facts about tourmaline is that its specific gravity varies with its color, although generally it is not a heavy stone. Some specimens have a cat's-eye effect and are cut to display the resultant chatoyancy. The characteristics of this stone are as follows: The hardness varies from 7.0 to 7.5; making it the equivalent of garnet on this scale. It is fairly light, with a specific gravity rating of 2.98 to 3.20. Its luster is glassy. Its color varies greatly with different colors in the same crystal. Tourmaline has a simple composition with only two elements, aluminum and silica, present in its molecules.

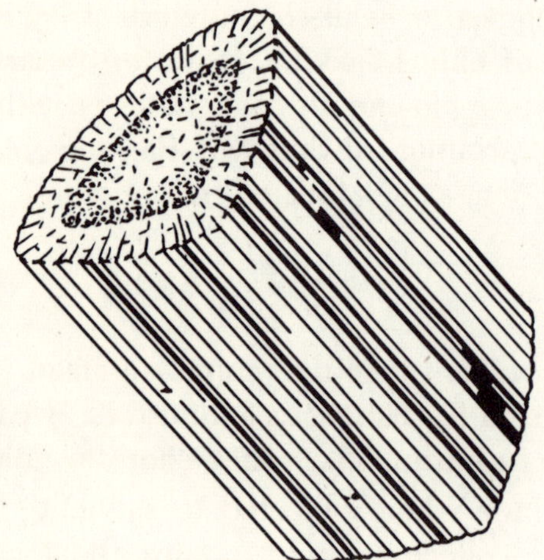

FIGURE 9. TOURMALINE CRYSTAL

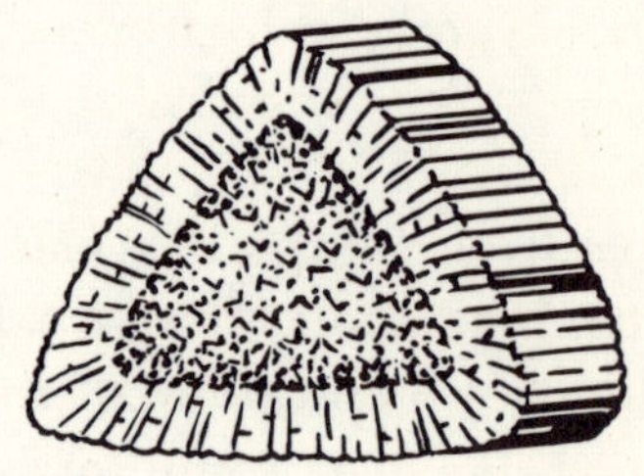

Turquoise and other copper gems. Turquoise, although an opaque gemstone, has been a favorite jewel all over the world from prehistoric times. It was as popular in the Egyptian and Persian civilizations as it was among the American Indians. The origin of the name of the gem is interesting. As it reached Europe by way of Turkey, it was called *turquoise* which is the French equivalent of Turkey. It ranges in color from sky blue to green. The sky-blue color is generally preferred, but some lovely specimens of bluish green delicately veined by the brown matrix are cherished. By matrix we mean the rock in which a gem is found. While the large deposits in New Mexico are mostly depleted, new mines are constantly being discovered in Nevada. Turquoise is porous and must be protected from oil, moisture and dirt. It is widely used in cabochoned settings and is very popular in brooches, earrings, pendants, necklaces and rings. It has a very complex chemical structure. Its characteristics are: Turquoise has a hardness of 6 on the Mohs scale. It is quite light when lifted, with a specific gravity of 2.60 to 2.83. It has a waxy luster. Its color varies from blue through blue-green to green. It may be somewhat chalky, but, if so, one usually has in hand an inferior specimen. Its chemical components are copper, oxygen, aluminum, phosphorus, hydrogen and oxygen.

Three other copper gem materials are azurite, malachite and chrysocolla. Azurite is azure blue, malachite is bright green and chrysocolla varies from green to greenish blue. These three opaque stones are almost always located in the upper levels of copper mines. Chrysocolla looks much like turquoise, but can be distinguished from it because it is much softer, having a hardness factor of only 2.4.

This chapter is the beginning of a classification of precious and semiprecious stones. The author recommends that the reader pause after finishing this chapter and do some field work in various museums or rock shops. He should not return to the book until he has familiarized himself with these crystals so that he feels in command of this material. He will find as soon as he reaches a museum or rock shop that there are a great many exhibits that have not been mentioned in this chapter. There are many subclassifications of gems and these he can acquire later. But to be able to identify these few rocks at the beginning gives a solid basis for his initial introduction. Other learning may be based on this information.

3. How Do You Find Gems?

ARE YOU WONDERING about the title of this chapter? After all, we have described the particular geological formations where you might locate gems. But that is general background, and we need to be very specific. This can be proved by listening to the "learning experiences" of any rockhound. Six years ago a friend of ours developed an overwhelming desire to dig fire opal for a few days. He carefully assessed all the places that were within a thousand miles. Then he talked with some of his collecting friends about the quality of the fire opal in various locations and their accessibility. He found that there is fire opal in a certain section of Nevada. However, those mines proved to be commercial and no access was permitted. So he narrowed the choice down to a mine in Idaho that had recently produced some excellent specimens. Other collectors had been there and were pleased with the attitude of the owner. Our friend plotted his course on the map and duly set out to achieve his goal. He drove all the way to Idaho without mishap, found the locality without trouble, and then, at the gate to the mine, was told that the owner had decided to mine the holding himself and was not allowing anyone in. Fortunately our friend had some other digging targets on that trip and all was not lost, but he figured that he had traveled about five hundred miles and lost two days in a futile and frustrating experience.

Inquire First

The first rule that many rockhounds follow is never to make a long trip to a listed locality without first inquiring about its present production and availability. How do you do that? First, you contact members of rock clubs or mineral clubs to see if any person in your area has actually investigated the site. Rockhounds are eager to share their experience. This is one excellent reason to join a local as well as a state gem and mineralogical association. The availability of individuals who have explored digging sites does two things: First, they provide the best source of information about the productivity of an area and, second, they help to pinpoint the precise location. This also presents the rockhound with an opportunity to learn something about local conditions. I was most fortunate before I left on a collecting trip to Colorado to learn from a native of that state that a great many of the digging sites are above ten thousand feet in altitude. The list of gems available in Colorado is intriguing, but when one learns that much of the material is obtainable only at locations above ten thousand feet and, even worse, in difficult terrain one tempers one's enthusiasm in terms of one's physical condition. I have some beautiful topaz and smoky quartz specimens from Colorado, but some of my other targets were regretfully dismissed.

In planning trips it is wise to discover not only the altitude, but the degree of effort required to be productive. A great many individuals who sit for eleven months in an office should not climb to 11,000 feet and swing a pick all day. Older individuals must temper their love for a particular gem with a realistic appraisal of the way in which their physical condition matches the requirements of the site. We have one tailing pile at the El Dorado (and we are not at all high in elevation—about the same elevation as Salt Lake City) that is named for a man who had just begun to dig and then had suffered a fatal heart attack. In running our particular mine we are very careful to suggest that everyone start gently and acclimate himself to the real work that is involved in digging, screening and washing the ore for sapphires. Of course this is no novel approach to exercise. Doctors have long talked about the need to condition oneself for any physical exertion whether it be tennis, golf or a new young wife. There are certain times of the year when digging in and around the great deserts of Nevada is enjoyable and rewarding; there are other times when one assiduously avoids both the heat and the sidewinders. Very specific information is needed about the availability of the site for digging, the conditions under which digging may occur, and the ways to find a particular site. For this, other experienced rockhounds are a generally reliable source of information.

A second accurate source is the local lapidary shop. In most communities shop owners spend hours gossiping with their clients about the productivity of this area or that and the trials and tribulations of the effort. While not the final word, one does take seriously the owner of a store when he says, "Hell, that area has been dead for years. Last year Ben Jones and later Mrs. Smith went. . . ." Many rockshop proprietors cut or mount the gems brought back by their clients and they usually have a great deal of firsthand information regarding many sites.

Just as rewarding is contact in person or by mail with the owner of the rockshop in the vicinity of the site to be explored. He will usually give a direct and candid answer to questions regarding any complications involved in prospecting there. Many store owners know of new and more recent finds which they are glad to share with the rockhound who writes an intelligent letter of inquiry to them. A list of such shops is carried once a year by the *Lapidary Journal* and this alone makes a subscription to that journal a quite valuable investment.

When I visit an area that has been recommended by the local rockshop owner I invariably make it a point to visit him, thank him and buy a few specimens while there. My purchase of specimens enables him to continue as a resource for rockhounds, but it also does something else. In many cases the gem that appears in a book looks quite different when seen in the field. It may have been altered on the surface so that what one needs to recognize is not the gem, but the *appearance of the gem in that locality*. It is an entirely different thing to see a cabochoned moss agate from Montana and the moss agate in the field. In the field it is most often covered with a crust of white or gray limestone or alkali-looking material. Once the collector is familiar with this appearance it helps enormously to spot the agate. The rockshop owner has local stones in abundance, so inspecting and buying a few of these helps greatly. It may be that a garnet is a garnet is a garnet, but anyone who has even randomly dug for garnets know that they come in astonishingly different varieties of form, color and presentation. Of course most rock dealers are enthusiastic about their local rocks.

A further useful source of information is the local chamber of commerce. Many of these associations are concerned with tourist trade and they go to great trouble to answer letters of inquiry regarding the resources in the community. I have seldom written to a chamber of commerce without receiving a prompt response that contained answers to my questions along with a detailed map giving directions to mining locations. The following questions in letters to chambers of commerce have proved valuable:

1. Is the mining facility open? At what hours? At what cost?
2. What are the camping facilities?
3. What is the weather generally like at the time of the projected visit?
4. Is there a local rock club in the community? If so, may I have the name and address of the president and secretary?
5. Where is the nearest rockshop? Name and address?
6. What other collecting opportunities are there in the area in addition to the ones I have mentioned?
7. Have there been any recent local or national mimeographed reports about the minerals in the area?

Answers to these questions will generally give enough information (or at least sources for further information) to enable me to make a decision as to whether to attempt a field trip to that locality. If inquiry indicated that there was a rich collecting area in Wyoming for petrified wood, but it could only be reached by Jeep; and I did not have a Jeep and could not rent one there was no sense in including that field in one's itinerary.

An additional resource covering most recent discoveries of significant digging areas is either *Gems and Minerals* or the *Lapidary Journal.* By the time a book has been written, edited and published it is already somewhat out of date. A subscription to either of these journals is richly rewarding in many ways but one dividend in particular is the vigilance of the editors to report on new finds. A map showing specific locations is generally included. Accompanying stories carry information regarding the quality of gem material, methods of mining, costs, camping facilities along with other significant details. There are often pictures to help familiarize the reader with the gem and the locality.

Where to Dig

Given this information about an area, the collector will want to know the most useful places to dig once he has arrived at a site. This he can learn from mine owners, from other diggers or from rockshop proprietors. Still it is wise to know something about the places one can most fruitfully collect. If he is digging for heavy gems such as garnet, ruby or sapphire the collector knows that in most areas (with the exception of the Yogo mine in central Montana) the dikes that contained these gems have long ago washed or eroded away and the gems have been carried off by streams. They are very heavy and therefore soon sink to the bedrock. So, if one were exploring a placer mine—a mine that is worked by washing away the material under a directed stream of water—one would explore the walls of the pit at the bedrock level. However, much topsoil has run down from the top during the years and produced a slope, as A in Chart III. Not until the wall has been made perpendicular by digging away the slope can one determine whether or not there are valuable gems left in the virgin ground not mined. (See B, Chart III.) This admonition seems important because in inspecting placer areas one

CHART III

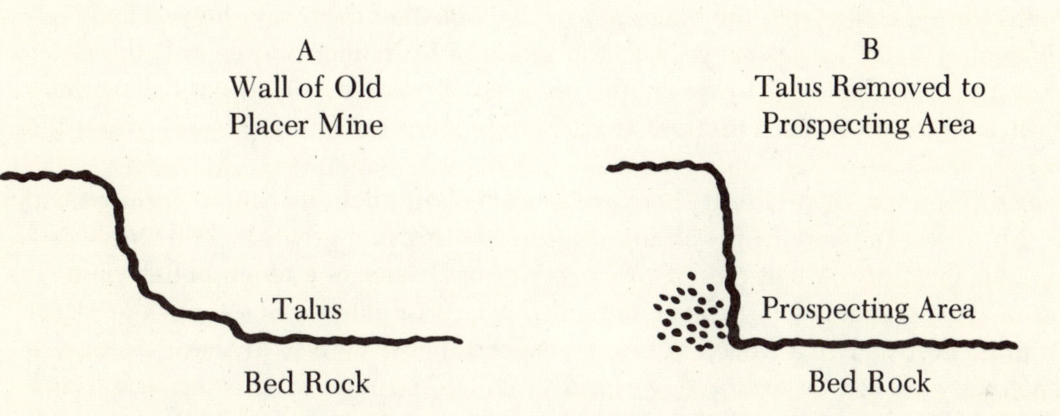

encounters hundreds of explorations in the talus which never reached the real virgin ground. Consequently the superficial excavations were fruitless. There are gems in the virgin ground in many of these. Of course one always explores the talus pile itself because it may contain gems which have come from dikes or sills higher on the wall. If there are specimens in the talus they may be abundant enough to justify screening the whole talus pile. Or they may lead to a careful exploration of the wall itself, because if there are gems on the talus they must have come from the wall. If the exploration proves rewarding one then moves along the wall and repeats the experiment to see how extensive the productive virgin ground may be.

In placer mining, "islands" are often left in the center of the mine. These need to be carefully investigated. They may be only piles of large rock which was thrown there or they may be genuine areas of virgin ground that could not be reached because of the particular placement of the water source. Much gold and not a few gems have been recovered from these islands.

Next, one explores the area around the sluice boxes. Sluice boxes are imperfect at best and many specimens have been recovered under and around the places where sluice boxes were located. These can be pinpointed with some accuracy because of the location of the tailing piles. Many remnants are still in place. At the El Dorado Mine the Chinese regarded the sapphires as a great nuisance because they clogged the riffles on the sluices. So they scooped the sapphires up and threw them away. This procedure is probably the explanation of several of the glory holes that have been reported at various mines.

After one has explored all the area around the cut in the hill where the sluice box was located, one moves next to study the tailing pile below. In early mines the operators were unaware of the value of mineral specimens or gems and simply let them escape with the other rocks. Thus, in many cases the tailing pile will be as rich as the virgin ground and the gems will be fairly well distributed. However, the surface of the tailing pile may be fairly unrewarding for two good reasons: Over the years the heavy gems, being quite small, may have worked their way down some distance, and, secondly, the surface of the tailing pile is the last to be completed and may represent the least valuable ore because it came from the boundary of the mine that the assay showed had high mineralogical content. In my experience the section of a tailing pile nearest the sluice box is the most productive. However, this may not be universally true. Tailing piles are not difficult to screen because they are generally a loose mixture of sand, rocks and gems.

Areas differ in productivity. If there are many tailing piles and much virgin ground it pays to prospect the various possibilities before putting in a great deal of time working on one or the other. A half day of prospecting may result in a much better yield.

Seasoned rockhounds will explore several other possibilities. Sometimes the placer miners ran their ore down a trench before it reached the sluice box. If there are dips in that trench they should be explored. Several years ago I found such a dip in a trench and reasoned that sapphires had undoubtedly sunk to the bottom and lodged there. It took me a day and a half to excavate the dip, but I was rewarded by a unique seven-carat chartreuse sapphire. Ledges in the trenches and on the sides of the walls may well be investigated, for these often hold good gems. Also, areas around processing plants and mine headquarters sometimes produce good specimens.

What about other types of underground mines? Stay out of them unless you have a guide who knows the mine. Many of them have bad timbers, bad air, bad reptiles, loose rocks and slippery terrain. They are often the home of black widows, rattlesnakes and scorpions. The lighting is poor and one can easily slip and sustain a fracture. The timbers are often rotten and the slightest jar can dislodge walls and ceiling so that one is in danger of being engulfed or imprisoned. After one has been in such a mine and heard a slide between himself and the opening one learns to be very cautious.

Some of the very same precautions must be taken in another good hunting area, *rock quarries*. Some of our best finds of gems, mineral specimens and fossils have come from quarries. They are open and accessible but the walls often are in extremely poor shape. One should always investigate the edge at the top of any wall he is going to explore to make sure there is not a precariously balanced rock above his head. One should also explore the surface to see whether the mining operation has badly cracked any section that might give way above him or underneath him. Collecting at rock quarries can be done in the debris at the bottom, in the piles of rock already quarried, and on the walls themselves. Generally, permission must be obtained from the operator of a quarry before one is permitted to hunt there.

Road cuts were first brought to my attention twenty years ago when I was driving on a new road in the area of Custer, Wyoming. I was 50 feet beyond the site when I realized that the road had been cut straight through a massive 20-foot-high vein of rose quartz. Needless to say I hunted first for a safe parking spot and then spent the next five hours accumulating some excellent specimens of rose quartz. I recently had a similar experience in southern Idaho. I was loafing along, enjoying a new road, when I went through a cut that contained thousands of geodes. I collected a bagful, but they were very light and I suspected they were hollow. Most of them did prove to be hollow, but to my delight I discovered that they glowed beautifully under the black light, so the stop was worthwhile. If there is one thing the rockhound learns, it is to keep his eyes open no matter where he is. There are many tales like the one about the discovery of some fine chiastolite crystal found just behind the Beverly Hills Hotel in Beverly Hills, California.

Of course one always looks for pegmatite dikes when one is in an area known for its high mineralized content. Dikes and veins come in all sizes. Some are a few inches wide and others are several feet. If one follows a dike or vein it may suddenly expand in size and contain several vugs (cavities) that hold good crystals. All of the dike should be carefully explored because the area (called the "contact zone") between the dike material and the other rock often produces valuable gems.

As one explores areas known to have produced gems and looks up at the hills one occasionally sees outcrops in which very hard rock has successfully resisted erosion. These are often the source of minerals and gems. Quartz outcroppings should be inspected very carefully because they may bear many minerals and crystals.

If one looks across the desert floor one is aware of a great many smaller or larger rocks that have been dislodged from the hills and carried by water and gravity away from the slopes. This material is called float. It gives a clue to what is in the hills, but it may also produce some excellent specimens on its own. Float in streambeds and below massive hills is an excellent source of both information and stones.

One further place to look for specimens is on roadbeds. I found an excellent source of garnets in Idaho simply because I was attracted to some red pebbles in the road. I remember that at one mine the owner had flattened out one area for parking. Sitting idly on the parking lot I let my eye roam beneath me and discovered several good specimens at my feet. I found out later that the parking spot had been made from a very old tailing pile. And I remember squatting down on a road to discuss digging with Bill Eaton when he casually reached down and picked up an almost perfect green sapphire crystal out of the roadbed.

Plowed fields are often good spots to look for agate or other stones when the fields lie in valleys. It is assumed that much of the material has worked its way down into the valley. This is particularly true of Montana moss agate. The Yellowstone River has been extensively worked over, the gravel dumps are carefully searched by local rockhounds, and the streambeds that are tributaries to the Yellowstone, which used to abound in agate, have few left. But every spring a goodly number of moss agates are turned up in the fields of eastern Montana. If one can be there at the right time and gain permission of the rancher to walk his fields fine specimens can still be obtained. This is also true of hunting for arrow or spear heads if one includes this hobby with rockhunting.

Areas around extinct volcanoes are often rich in mineralized matter. The gem material will be found in cavities and cracks in the lava where the gases and heat of the lava interacted with the sedimentary rock on which it flowed to produce crystal structures. The thunder egg (chalcedony in rounded nodule) was formed in some such fashion. The fire opal of Nevada is believed to be metamorphosized volcanic ash. Much opalized wood is the product of lava flows. Consequently the prospector who knows extinct volcanic areas does well to inspect such areas carefully. The author has dug successfully in many ash beds for geodes in Nevada. A cylindrical cast of a tree or branch that has been replaced by opal, quartz or chalcedony is a valuable specimen.

The beaches of lakes and oceans can be quite productive. The highly prized Lake Superior agate is found in good quantities on some of the shores of smaller lakes in northern Minnesota and Wisconsin and of course on the shores of Lake Superior. One has no difficulty in finding a small bagful of excellent specimens on the shores of Lake Superior not far out of Duluth itself. Excellent agate is found on some of the beaches in Monterey County in California, moonstones on the beaches of Southern California, and a profusion of agates up and down the whole Pacific Coast, although the best results are obtained on the Oregon beaches.

Clustering

Perhaps the most important consideration in planning a field trip is to coordinate information in such a way as to make it possible to visit a maximum number of areas in the shortest amount of time. When one has accumulated the essential information about the location and conditions surrounding each target area the next task is to put all of this together in a rational plan. For instance, if you were to plan a trip to Montana and your goal was to gather opals, moss agates, garnets and sapphires you would stop first at Spencer at the border of Idaho and Montana, move from there 100 miles to the area of Ruby Lake, then north another 100 miles to the El Dorado sapphire mine at Helena, Montana, and finally directly east on Highway 10 to the agate grounds in eastern Montana.

A good trip plan should take one logically from one site to another, as well as including museums, parks, and enough spare time to visit any rich field you may hear about on the trip. One plans efficiently but leisurely so that there will be ample time to travel and rest in between collecting stops. If you acquire or take along books on the wildflowers, geology, and wildlife of the area, and the location of mining spots you will add to your enjoyment. Such a trip is truly recreation, and an education besides.

Books

Although rockhounding may be new to you, it is not a new hobby in America. Thousands of persons have traveled into every nook and cranny of our country in the search for precious and semiprecious gems. Their experience is recorded in a great many helpful books. Many of these books present specific maps of the different areas in several states so that clustering is already achieved for the rockhound. The wealth of information they present is a very good bargain. The Gem Trails in this country are well traveled and well documented. Before the novice starts out on his first expedition he will do well to study books about his particular state or the state he wishes to explore. Rock shops and most mineralogical museums have a rack of such books that are a very good investment.

4. How Do You Dig for Gems . . . and With What?

THE LAST CHAPTER described some of the pitfalls of hunting for gems and made concrete suggestions about ways in which to locate rewarding gem fields. We now assume that you have arrived and are looking over the site. This chapter deals with the specific ways in which ore is recovered and gems isolated from the ore. It is a great sadness to see so many persons pour scores of gems out of their screens or leave remarkable specimens behind. Try as we will, many individuals do not follow instructions, and leave their digging with half the material they should have recovered still on the ground. We will talk first about the standard equipment which facilitates maximum yield.

Figure 10 shows most of the equipment that you will need for any digging operation. Of course there are special circumstances in which even these tools will not suffice, but in general these are the essential items to obtain before you set out. We list them and then, in discussing various types of digging, we will describe how they are used. The essential items are:

1. Rock pick.
2. Large miner's pick.
3. Crowbar.
4. One or two long bars.
5. Several cold chisels of varying length. (Sharpened leaves from old car springs are also very useful.)
6. Short hand-shovel.
7. Medium-length digging shovel.
8. Long-handled shovel.
9. Long-handled L-shaped curved bar as illustrated.
10. Small sledgehammer.
11. Two sifting screens—one with ½-inch mesh and the other with ¼-inch mesh.
12. Gold pan.
13. Large broom and a whiskbroom.
14. Large tarpaulin.
15. Safety eyeglasses, or goggles.
16. Magnifying glass.
17. Several large pails, a knapsack and gunnysacks.
18. Collection of pennies, files, quartz, etc., to test hardness.
19. Plastic bottles to contain the smaller gems.

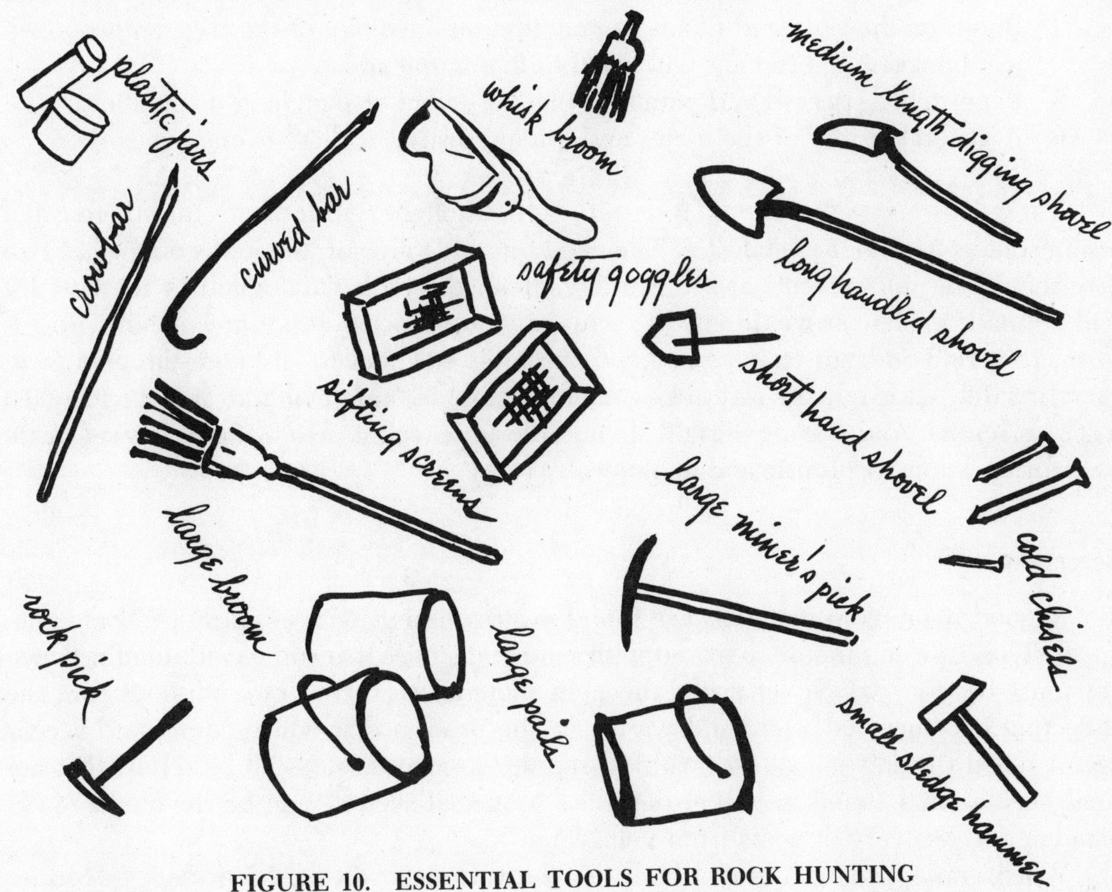

FIGURE 10. ESSENTIAL TOOLS FOR ROCK HUNTING

Just as important are the following accessories not directly involved in digging, but which make the digging more comfortable and safer:

1. Snake kit.
2. Pair of heavy boots.
3. Pair of wading boots.
4. Serviceable work clothes.
5. Several pairs of heavy gloves.
6. Several bottles of insect repellent.
7. Extra containers of gasoline and water.
8. A powerful flashlight.
9. Sleeping bag, cot, Coleman stove, dishes.

To add extra dimension to the field trip, the following items will enhance your enjoyment of the whole trip:

1. A good camera and lots of film.
2. A pair of binoculars.
3. All the recent gem books available on the locality you are planning to visit.

4. Books on the flora and fauna, animal life, and geology of the area, anthropological books on the Indians who used to live in the area.
5. Paper tablet, pencils and paints (if one has talent at sketching or painting).
6. A general history of the mines and mining district if there is one available.

These lists may seem formidable but a little thought will indicate that there is not a superfluous item in the catalogue. The need for, and value of, the items on the last two lists should be self-evident, and the utility of all the tools catalogued in the first list will be made evident as we discuss the actual digging process. It is a melancholy process to make a find and not to have at hand the tools essential to dislodge the gem or to carry it safely. It is equally sad to be uncomfortable in one's living arrangements when rest is essential. And it is downright deplorable to leave an area without having made an effort to know its historic and geological secrets.

Screening

A good many gem materials are found in stream beds, gravel piles or volcanic deposits. These are commonly so mixed with sand and stones that some method of processing must be used which separates the gem material from the ore. Without this, the collecting becomes inefficient and wasteful. The process that will be described here is useful when digging for garnets, rubies, sapphires, agates, etc.—all materials that are small, heavy, and found in gravel deposits. A special section will be devoted to gold panning and recovery of gems from veins later.

When you approach a gravel bed, test the various levels of the present or former stream banks to determine the location of gem deposits. That deposit is most likely to occur near the bedrock of the present or past stream bed. Judicious testing will often reveal, however, that, while there is a major concentration at the lower levels, other dikes were washed out at different times and thus there are some concentrations at other levels. Having located the gems and their associated minerals (like hematite in the case of sapphires), one then moves to transform the material gathered from simply a deposit to ore. By *ore* we mean a concentration of the deposit material into the size ore that would include all the minerals sought. The specific size is thus determined by the largest known example of the gem under consideration.

To concentrate the gravel into the right size of ore requires three operations. The first operation is to extract the ore material from a bank, stream bed, or whatever. This generally is not too difficult, because the gravel deposits are usually quite loose and not tightly packed. There are times, however, when the pressure of the deposit itself and the chemical action of the moisture have concretized the layer of ore that lies closest to the bedrock. It is essential to dig out this layer of ore because very often the best specimens have been captured in this hard material. It must be somewhat laboriously picked out in hard chunks and these must be broken up in order to free the gems. However, this must be done with some caution lest heavy sledgehammer or pick blows fracture any gems held in the material. Generally this can be done by placing the ore on a large smooth rock with a declivity in the middle and, using the big pick as a tamp, gently begin tamping the body. If it does not crumble, harder blows will be needed, but one should not hit the material with more force than necessary because good gems are often ruined in this way.

Gravel material comes in all sizes and shapes and often large boulders are encountered. If these boulders lie on the bedrock they present a formidable obstacle to further digging. However, they also present a remarkable opportunity. Large specimens often are arrested by large stones, so it is well to clear off the bank above the stone and work down around it carefully in order that no material will be lost. When the stone is free it can be moved by using the long straight bar as a lever. In moving it care should be taken, however, to see that all the material above and around it is removed so that none will be lost. Ore material will generally cling to such a rock and must be wiped or chipped off because these encrusted adherences may contain some of the best gems. When the rock has been removed and cleaned, the area where it lay should be carefully gathered in order to be screened later. The digger must always determine the direction of flow of the stream or, if it is a dry stream, the direction in which it once flowed, so that he will be able to locate any pockets around the rock carried there by the stream. The whole area around the stone should be cleaned.

A word of advice is essential here. The course of bedrock is never smooth. It rises and falls and often contains many riffles. These ought always to be cleaned off carefully with the pick end of the rock hammer. After they are loosened, the area should be swept with a whisk broom to be sure that all the ore material is recovered. Generally it is wise to remove several inches of the bedrock because many gems of considerable size often work themselves down into the bedrock and will not be recovered unless this top half inch is cleaned out, crushed and screened. No one ought to leave a digging site unless it looks as clean as a kitchen floor just after waxing. It is the common practice of proprietors of gem mines to recommend this procedure, but their advice is seldom followed. If one is digging for several days, at the end of each day the entire digging area ought to be swept to recover any gems that may have fallen down from the side of the bank or been fortuitously dislodged from the bedrock.

In the gravel beds one often encounters stumps of trees long since dead. These areas should be excavated with extraordinary care because gems tend to accumulate around the root cavities as the tree rots. This is the reason that in a digging area one will find many excavations around large trees or tree roots. However, the merit of excavating around living trees is a debatable point. We have made a rule in our mine that no one may dig closer than ten feet to a living tree. Of course we have sufficient digging area so that to ruin a tree is unnecessary. However, the wanton destruction of trees in digging areas and around old mines has made these areas places of devastation and it is hoped that in the future miners will be more considerate of vegetation than they have been. This is not to say that digging around stumps is not a valuable exercise. It is not easy to dig with a pick among roots that have not rotted, but those who have experience in such matters would rather expend the effort than to dig in less productive spots.

We have said to pay particular attention to declivities in the bedrock (particularly

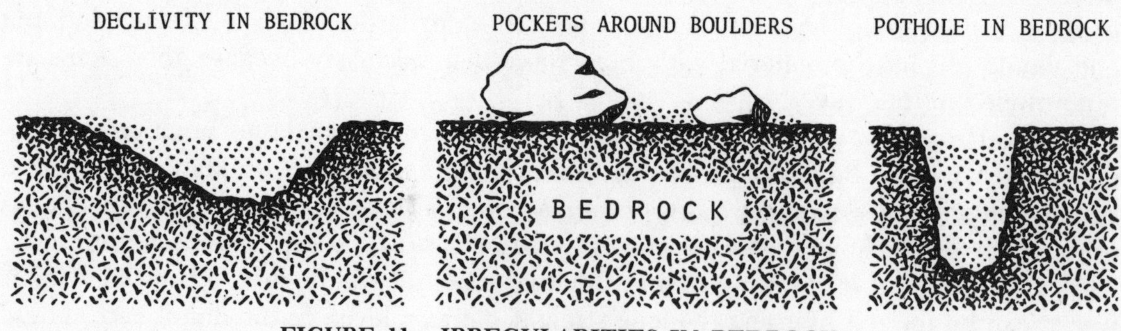

FIGURE 11. IRREGULARITIES IN BEDROCK

when there are riffles), to areas around huge boulders, and to spots around tree stumps. There is one other kind of area that has proved to have fabulous deposits, and that is potholes. Potholes will not generally be discovered unless one is following the bedrock. When one is found, it may literally be filled with gems, but these may be cracked and broken depending on the force of the water, the size of the pothole, etc. Some of the peculiar shapes of the bedrock are illustrated in Figure 11.

When you come to one of the mines where a great many persons have worked in the past you will generally find that it has been some time since anyone has dug in the spot and that there will be considerable fall-in or debris in the bottom. This must be cleaned out and screened because part of it may have fallen from gem-bearing layers of the site.

The experienced miner never tunnels because (*a*) it is not fair to the person who follows and (*b*) it is exceptionally dangerous. Every mine in existence (and even some of those where individuals are digging in river or stream banks where they have good visibility and access) has sad memories of miners who were killed or maimed because they insisted on tunneling. We do not permit tunneling at our mine and most careful operators try to protect those who dig in their holdings by prohibiting it. Tunneling is a most inefficient way of mining also, because once a certain depth of hole has been reached it is impossible to go farther without stopping and spending a long time clearing out the overburden. It is far better to take the overburden off as one goes along. For that purpose a strong tarp is invaluable. One carefully puts the tarp down with several inches curled up on the bank to prevent gravel from piling up underneath it. Then one picks off the overburden onto the tarp and when a sufficient amount (not too heavy) is on the tarp its four corners are gathered together and the tarp is dragged away. The process is repeated until the bank slopes backward. One is then in position to dig all the gem-bearing ore with relative ease. Some miners leave the tarp on the ground when the bank is being dug so that nothing that has been dug out will escape.

The advantages of using the tarp are that it is a more efficient and not as difficult way as shoveling the material and there is better control of the gravel with not so much gem-bearing ore being thrown away.

Let us suppose that one has cleared away the overburden and is ready to process the ore. The first thing to be done is to again clear away any large rocks that hang above . . . for safety's sake. Then any large rocks in the ore-bearing material are thrown out. Finally the gravel or dirt (already partly refined because of throwing out the larger stones by hand) is shoveled into the first of two screens. If one is using a standard screen it will have ½-inch mesh. Enough ore is shoveled into the screen so that it is not too heavy to manipulate but full enough so that the operation is efficient. Then the screen is swished back and forth with a rhythmic motion. If one keeps his back straight and learns to swing the screen with a good rhythm the operation is not nearly so tiring as when the back is bent over and the motion is jerky. The operation is confined to an area above the second screen. It is possible to do this operation in a simpler way which takes much less energy and which many older persons use. The first screen with the larger mesh is placed on the second screen and the ore is moved back and forth by hand until all the smaller stones have fallen into the second screen.

In either case when the operation is over the first screen is dumped. However, it is always wise to look over the contents of the larger screen just in case a very large crystal did not go through the ½-inch mesh. The second screen with ⅛- or ¼-inch mesh (the size depends on the size of gems the miner wishes to save) is now lifted and swung back and forth in the same rhythmic manner. As all the ore that you desire to retain will be kept in this screen it does not matter where the sand, dirt and small particles go. Thus, there is more freedom of movement in processing the ore this second time. It is wise, however, to do this screening in the same place and to build a pile of sand or dirt. A reason for this is that the sand may be rich in black sand and gold, so that the miner may want to spend some time processing the sand after he has completed his search for crystals.

Before going on with the process of refining and processing the ore, let's say a word about the disposal of the large stones, the larger gravel from the first screening, and the sand or dirt from the second screening. In my early days of mining I spent many totally useless hours of shoveling because I had miscalculated how soon the tailings that were discarded would catch up with my digging. Far too many times that tailing pile grew behind me until it was intruding into the mine. By then it would be so large that I had to take many hours to move the whole tailing pile once more. It is always wise to carry the tailings screen by screen many feet away from the mine so that if one strikes a particularly rich section one will not imprison himself in tailings.

An even worse mistake is to dump those tailings on gravel that has not yet been touched. Some collectors, in their eagerness to get at gems, have no regard at all for the others who will follow them, and there is scarcely a digging site in which yards and yards of virgin ore or good gravel have not been foolishly covered by the tailings of individuals who were so eager to dig that they destroyed the site. About half of one huge tailing pile (the richest in the whole area) at the El Dorado is useless because diggers randomly threw tailings over very rich gravel that was to the left, to the right and behind them.

When the ore has been reduced to the size of stone that is wanted for washing, the screen is carefully emptied into a large pail, a knapsack or a gunnysack and the contents are stored until enough ore is accumulated to process. This ore is then taken to a lake, stream (or large water container if no body of water is available) and is poured out of the container into the fine screen. The screen is submerged in shallow water and carefully rubbed with the gloved hand. This is to remove all dirt from crystals so that they can be easily spotted. If the gems are very dirty this is a very important part of the process.

The screen is then carried to deeper water and is submerged to just the level of the ore. It is sharply rocked back and forth a number of times. The screen is then shifted in the hands until it is held on the opposite sides and it is sharply rocked again. This process is repeated four times. A good way to check this is simply to be sure that each of your hands holds each of the four sides of the screen before the procedure is finished. If the process is performed correctly all the crystals will be gathered in a small circle in the bottom of the screen. The screen is then taken out of the water and a place is selected on which to dump it. The area must be made very flat so that the ore will not run and cover any of the gems. It must also be in direct sunlight so the crystals may be seen. The last act in this manipulation is to flip the screen over so that the material on the bottom is now on the top.

The crystals are now picked out of the ore with tweezers and placed in a plastic bottle. This whole procedure of rocking the screen to gather the gems in the center and then of flipping the screen over carefully to bring the gems to the surface ought to be practiced assiduously with gravel taken from the beach or other tailings until it can be done efficiently and smoothly. Even then there will be screens at times that for some reason resist gathering to the center or "run" when flipped. In these cases it is always wise to scoop the ore up and repeat the whole process.

There are many individuals who, after washing and gathering, dump the screen on a white piece of linen or muslin and then laboriously go through the whole screen piece by piece so that they do not miss a single gem. This is generally a waste of time for someone who has learned to center his gems and to flip them accurately. A much more efficient way of guarding against loss is to "save the centers." By saving centers we mean taking the inner circle where the crystals appeared to a depth of several inches and tossing the center into an empty pail. Then, when the main task of washing the ore has been finished, the centers are rewashed. This is a worthwhile process and most careful miners use this procedure.

One cannot overemphasize how important skill is in washing the stone. After the hard work of picking out or shoveling the ore and screening it twice before washing it is nonsensical to use crude methods of gem recovery. Nevertheless, despite the pleas from experts, all manner of strange gyrations and contortions are seen on the washing beach and numbers of good gems are lost. Rescreening the tailing piles often results in the recovery of some excellent stones. While it may take a little practice to perfect the rocking and flipping operations, they can be mastered by anyone so that good recovery of crystals can be achieved. It does seem strange that some individuals who sweep their mines very carefully so as not to lose a single stone will use the most haphazard ways of washing when they get to the final operation.

Just as impossible to understand is dry screening. Many individuals never bother with water when digging crystals. They hold their screen up to the sunlight and if they do not see a gem through the bottom they throw the screenful away. Afterwards, one can find some splendid stones they missed. It is a fact that no one can dry screen efficiently. The crystals are too small and too easily obscured by other stones and sometimes far too dirty to be seen without washing.

The following daily schedule is the product of long experience. Most of us dig in late spring, summer or early fall when the weather is hot. Digging in the middle of the day is a piece of foolishness that no one ought to practice. One ought to get up early in the morning when it is cool and do the digging before eleven o'clock when the sun really becomes overpowering. Then one can repair to the stream or the lake, don boots and wash during the hours when it would be unbearable on the hillside or down in a hole. After washing it is time for a leisurely lunch, a nap or at least some good reading. About four or five o'clock one can return to dig again because it is cooler. The one problem is that many individuals race the clock, dig like mad, and then try to screen that night at dusk when the light is very poor. Those ores ought to be saved for the next day and screened along with the ore gathered the next morning. More gems will be recovered, one will have had a good rest, and the whole operation will be done in consonance with the temperature. One's irritability threshold also will be lower and production higher.

When one has finally recovered the gems they ought to be put in a *plastic* container. Somewhere in the mountains of Colorado there is a beautiful blue topaz that I will never see again because I used a glass container which I thought was plastic. It slipped out of my pocket, hit a rock and fractured. The contents flew in all directions. I recovered most of it, but that one beautiful gem could not be found before dark. Pockets, paper bags, pans, and even fruit jars are continually used at digging spots. I faithfully carry with me on all trips dozens of extra plastic bottles so that I can share them with others. It hurts me too much to see (as I have every summer for twenty-five years) a glass container smashed and gems lost forever. If one is going to dig in the same place for several days and is going to return another time it is important to label each plastic bottle as to where its contents were obtained. One learns to be discriminating when one site produces six gems and another six hundred. There is one final word about a plastic container. Keep it in a well-closed pocket or in a special pail with a lid or somewhere where it cannot be lost. It is easy to shovel dirt over a container or to lose it because it is so small. A friend of mine was humiliated many years ago when a miner came swinging down the trail with a plastic bottle and asked him if it were his. He had had it stuck in the sand tailings at his mine. He looked in the tailings and, sure enough, his container was gone. The visitor said that he had heard a rattle that sounded like sapphires while he was digging. He stopped and looked and there, scurrying along, was a ground squirrel with a plastic bottle in his mouth. The miner threw a rock at the squirrel and the squirrel dropped the bottle and ran away. So the miner went to look for the owner. My friend knew the container was his because it had a pink sapphire that was the best stone he had found in two weeks of digging! Incidentally, that honest and unselfish act of the miner is typical of the breed of men and women who call themselves rockhounds.

Dikes and Veins

Let us suppose you are in an area which has high mineralization and there are abundant signs that much digging has been done. You will probably be able to follow the pegmatite dike or sill and determine whether or not it was carefully explored throughout its whole length. If the entire dike or sill has been exploited, it is wise to move around in the area and discover the tailings that came from that area. If there are no large stones present it may be sufficient to use a ¼- or ⅛-inch screen to process the tailings. However, if you do not recover any crystals after repeatedly screening different layers and depths of the tailing pile it is wise to desist and try other tailing piles. It is particularly valuable to find tailings that are so grown over that it is apparent nobody has worked them for a long time. Again, if no crystals are recovered do not waste any more time because you may be screening only overburden although you should at that stage be able to recognize pegmatite rock and not waste time on simple dirt. If you begin to recover good crystals then you may indeed find more payload there than by digging in the original dike which probably was well cleaned out.

However, if you do not find any crystals in the dump piles this is no reason to abandon the area. Plot a course and hike around that pegmatite dike looking for others or for outcroppings. You may very well find another untouched dike or sill to be explored or you may find other tailing piles which, because they were more inaccessible or hidden by brush, have not been screened. You may examine these tailings in relationship to the pegmatite dike and discover that the section of the dike most likely to have produced crystals was not explored at all. One should know something of the signs that lead to the discovery of pockets of crystals.

One clue comes from a routine report on the Yogo sapphire mine in Montana. This early report stated that the heaviest mineralization—that is, the presence of sapphire crystals—occurred in greatest frequency where the dike was widest. One looks for pockets of crystals, therefore, in the center of the thickest portion of the pegmatite. If the pegmatite spreads or "bulges" this is a most likely spot to investigate other signs. Another sign of pockets is a surface resistance that is weak; in other words the material is softer than the surrounding pegmatite material. Furthermore there are apt to be numerous cracks spreading out from the pockets. Or a portion of the wall of the cavity of the pocket may already have rotted away, exposing a hollow space along the dike or sill. The original size of a pegmatite tells nothing about whether it contains mineralization or gems. Some small pegmatites may contain a series of small pockets with many specimens, while a much larger pegmatite in the same area may be barren. One other sign that helps locate pegmatites but says nothing about the mineralization of the pegmatite is the presence of quartz veins near by. These quartz veins may or may not contain some of the gem material found in a nearby pegmatite. The point is that quartz veins should alert one to the possibility of nearby dikes or sills, but do not guarantee their existence.

Suppose one has the good fortune to find a pegmatite sill which has not been disturbed or investigated by collectors. One follows it by digging away the topsoil until one has some notion of its extent. Then one begins a detailed look for any changes in thickness, any bulges, any area with spreading cracks or any place where it has weathered or eroded through so that cavities are exposed.

The central point at which cracks converge is to be very carefully explored. As one now may be on the point of uncovering very delicate crystals a small opening in the pocket is made. This is done as gently as possible so as not to fracture any fine crystals that grow from the point at which entrance itself is made. If there is a small opening already existing, the material lying on the floor of the cavity is extracted carefully and sifted for crystals. Then the strong flashlight mentioned earlier comes into play and the immediate walls of the pocket are explored.

When the floor is clean it is possible to see at least a part of the pocket and plans can be made for the recovery of crystals on the sides of the pocket. Because crystals that are recovered as they grew in matrix are much more valuable than single crystals, a series of gentle prying actions with the crowbar placed at the "contact" zone between the wall of the pocket and the pegmatite rock can split off pieces of the wall with crystals intact. The size of the aperture through which one works will be constantly increased until the whole pocket can be easily worked without damaging the crystals themselves. The cleaning-out process mentioned as the first step is continued throughout because if there is much material in the pocket the walls and crystals cannot be recovered or they will be damaged when forced against the material. Try to make the pocket empty at the place where one is prying out crystals. The collector who has this opportunity can afford to use infinite patience to work out his crystals without damaging them. When the pocket has been thoroughly cleaned out the pegmatite must be closely inspected for signs of other pockets and these possibilities explored.

It is just as important to protect crystal specimens as it is to have the proper containers for small crystal gems like garnets. If one has a knapsack to carry specimens down a hill it is important that enough newspaper or cloth be provided to wrap them securely so the bouncing nature of a walk to a vehicle will not destroy them. One may carry lots of newspaper or soft paper toweling or soft cotton cloth. The specimens are wrapped first in soft material and then wrapped again in paper. It is important to label specimens in terms of their exact location for further reference.

Digging

The rockhound may someday have the happy experience of discovering a large vein of rose quartz, plume agate, blue agate, or other material. Digging in a solid mass of agate is a quite different problem from digging out a pocket from pegmatite sills and dikes. The veins may be quite thick and in such pristine condition that it looks as though there are no cracks or pockets to make any headway in breaking away material for specimens. But this initial appearance may not be real, for if a vein is followed far enough there are breaks, fissures and cracks which can be used as a starting point to extract material. However, there are occasions when a particularly lovely piece of plume agate and rose quartz is situated in a large vein of agate which seems to have no openings of any kind into which to insert a sharp cold chisel. At that point one may be tempted simply to flail away at the rock hoping something will come off.

This is a destructive procedure! It is like smashing an encrusted moss agate with a heavy maul to see what is inside. It destroys the plume and rarely produces desirable specimens. At this point one has to inspect the vein very carefully to see whether it can be attacked from another side or from underneath, to see whether the large straight bar can be used to pry out any section of the vein or whether there is some kind of a declivity in which a chisel may be inserted and then pounded until a crack appears. When one crack is achieved, larger chisels can be inserted until a crowbar or straight bar can be inserted and enormous pressure exerted to pry out large enough sections to preserve the particular picture that has intrigued one.

This kind of heavy work is among the most dangerous in rockhounding and both the eyes and the hands must be carefully protected from the fragments of the hard rock that may fly toward the digger and also from the equally hard pieces of steel that may be chipped off by the heavy blows from the sledgehammer or the chisel. One of these buried itself so deep in the thumb bone of a friend of mine that it proved impossible to extract by probing and a minor operation was necessary to remove it.

Listening

Whether one is digging in the pipe for diamonds in Murfreesboro, Arkansas or in the bulldozed material at Spencer, Idaho, for fire opal it pays to listen to the advice given by those who are in charge. These people have long experience and they are interested in promoting the success of rockhounds who dig with them. How often a manager tries to help a newcomer in a digging area and that person indicates that he wishes to prospect in some other spot! Or an old hand who has worked an area for years offers kindly advice that is spurned by the novice. I remember clearing out our best digging bank for a rock club only to have one member tell the others that there was nothing there and then leading them to a nonproductive site that had been good some three years before. Of course they left with very little reward for much effort.

A productive spot for listening is around the campfire at night when the tales of the day are spun. After the novice has learned to identify likely signs he will be ready for prospecting, but in his first years he will do well to cultivate the gentle art of attentive listening.

5. What Do You Do With Gems?

THE PATHWAY THAT leads from being a collector of rocks and gems to being a skilled lapidary is long. But it does not seem long because each bend along the path reveals a new and richer vista with more intriguing activity. In this chapter we will spend much time on the first steps and then outline some of the possible achievements that can come later. The reason for this procedure is quite simple. We learn to crawl before we walk and we learn to run before we try a high jump.

Let us assume that you have done your homework and, having some sophistication about rocks and their recovery, you have just finished your first field trip. You made the trip on your vacation and brought home a half-bushel basket full of geodes, petrified wood, rose quartz, agate, jade and garnets. The other half of the basket is full of mysterious but attractive rock. What do you do with them?

Cleaning and Forming the Specimen

Before determining the value of a specimen it must be cleaned as well as possible so that one can see what it is like. Often specimens that are dull in the field and unpromising because of adhering matrix or chemical stains prove to be excellent prospects for mounting or faceting when they have been cleaned up. Other specimens that show great promise may prove to have too much chatoyance or too many minute fractures to process. Cleaning is the first task in the analysis of the value of any gems.

There are many ways to clean specimens. The most obvious is to wash them to eliminate as much dirt or grime as possible. When the material has soaked for a while, rendering the dirt soft, it is possible to use a paintbrush with long bristles or a toothbrush to work the clay or matrix from the sides of crystals. Very fine crystals require careful brushing so that none of their needlelike crystal formations will be damaged. The new jet spray may be effective in reaching small surfaces that cannot be easily stroked by a paintbrush or toothbrush. If the washing is thorough one can generally see enough of the specimen to determine how it should be treated to make it more attractive.

When the specimen is clean it is inspected. Poor color, deep scratches on the surface, a number of large or small fractures, inclusions of materials that are lumpy and poorly arranged or unattractive, or chatoyance that has no pattern (so that no brilliant point or star will appear), and cloudiness indicate to the collector that this particular specimen is not going to bring any gasps from his friends or an offer to trade from another rockhound. However at this point some judgment is required. It is often possible to grind off the scratches, to cut the stone in such a way that unsightly inclusions or "feathers" or areas that are cloudy can be eliminated. It is far better to have a small, brilliant stone than a larger one containing deficiencies that mar its loveliness.

Some stains can only be removed by acid immersion. A great deal of expertise is essential for this operation because (*a*) one must know what mineralogical matter is soluble in which acids and (*b*) acids are more harmful to skin than to minerals. Sinkankas has gone to the trouble of making a table of some 250 minerals and gems and indicating those that are dissolved or affected by the standard acids used for cleaning. If you do not have his book, ask about this at your local gem store.

When there is a certain artistic balance in any arrangement this adds considerably to its attractiveness. Small crystals of from one-half to one-and-one-half inches lose their impact when twice that depth of matrix is allowed to adhere to the crystal. Sometimes a group of particularly lovely crystals will include one that is fractured or ugly. In such a case it is wise to remove the odd crystal. Chipping away the matrix or an odd crystal must be done with enormous care, however, lest the entire specimen fragment. One wants a stable base on which the specimen will rest. This means that the bottom plane of the matrix must be leveled and smoothed. The collector will want to survey the specimen from many angles before he finally decides on the orientation he wants for his crystals. When the best angle of presentation is determined, he will then align his matrix so that the stone can be viewed from that angle.

We have discussed so far the forming of a crystal or group of crystals that will be exhibited as nature molded them. But some gems will need to be slabbed on a diamond saw to determine what treasures can be teased from the stone. Many collectors chip a

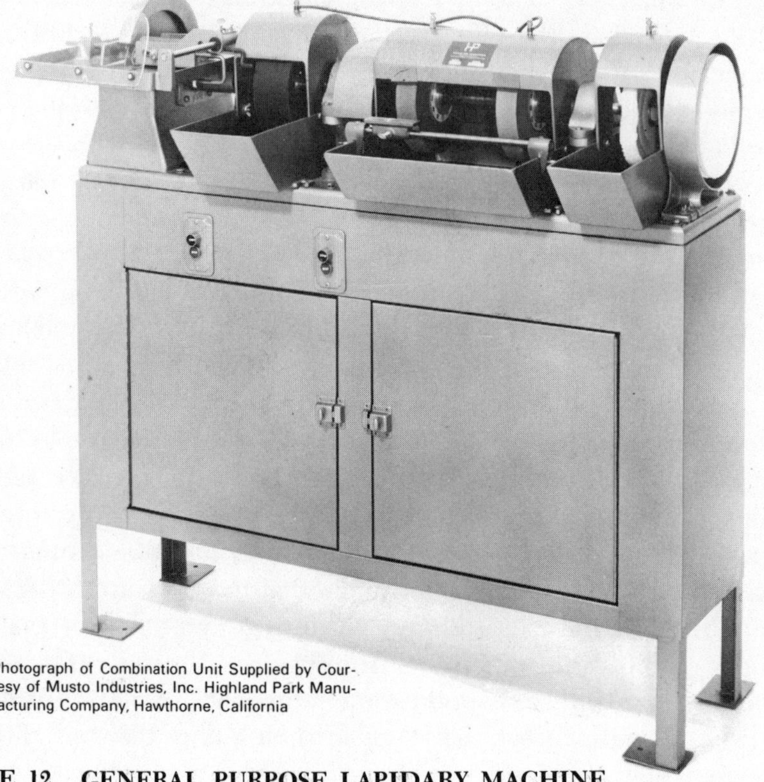

Photograph of Combination Unit Supplied by Courtesy of Musto Industries, Inc. Highland Park Manufacturing Company, Hawthorne, California

FIGURE 12. GENERAL PURPOSE LAPIDARY MACHINE

small piece of the stone on the collecting site to get some notion of its value before carrying the bulk all the way home. This is permissible, but specimens such as moss agate, plume agate, etc., vary so much that a small chip on one end may fail to reveal the promise on the other end. The collector ought to be quite conservative about this. He should carry home any specimen that looks at all promising. It is true, however, that some agates are perfectly clear and still are a waste as far as slabbing is concerned.

The collector's shop should be equipped with a very strong light for "candling" the specimen. This cannot be done well if there is a thick coating on the stone or if it is not clean. All stones should be thoroughly scrubbed before "candling." Then it is more likely that the collector will be able to see the inclusions, the bands, the pictures—all the things that are not visible by just holding the specimen to the light in the collecting area. If the collector is still in doubt a thin slice cut off each end by the diamond saw will enable him to see more adequately and to align his stone on the slabbing machine in such a way as to preserve the maximum beauty. At no time, either in the field or in the shop, should he ever simply hit the stone.

Beautiful finished pieces of jewelry are the result of planning, sawing, grinding, polishing and setting. Each of these steps requires appropriate tools.

Sawing

There are various types of saws used to cut stones. There are mud saws, abrasive saws, and diamond saws. But the diamond saw is the one generally used by most lapidaries so we will discuss the use of this saw. These saws are always circular and they may be purchased in any size from 1 inch to 24 inches, but the 8- to 12-inch saws are most popular. They are made of metal and the cutting edge is impregnated with small, sharp diamond particles. These saws are mounted on spindles and turned by electric motors. They are mounted on the spindle by themselves, together with a grinding wheel, or with grinding, sanding and polishing wheels. Figure 12 illustrates a general purpose lapidary machine with all necessary tools on one spindle.

Almost all diamond saws come equipped with a clamp to hold the rock that is to be sawed. This clamp runs on a plate designed to move parallel to the cutting wheel, thus making an accurate cut and preventing the damage to the saw blade that can occur if the rock shifts so that the saw blade is forced to bend. Quite small stones can be held by hand, but if they are to be sliced it is often necessary to embed them in plaster of paris in order not to waste any part of a good specimen.

Some diamond saws come equipped with a weight which is suspended beyond the saw and attached to the carriage holding the clamp by a cord that runs over a pulley. If the machine does not have it, this device can easily be constructed by filling a small tin can with about 5 pounds of rock. The advantage of this is that the steady pull of the weight guarantees a smooth cut. If the stone is pushed by hand differential pressure makes an uneven cut with consequent roughness on the specimen.

The friction of saw on rock produces heat which is damaging to the saw blade and

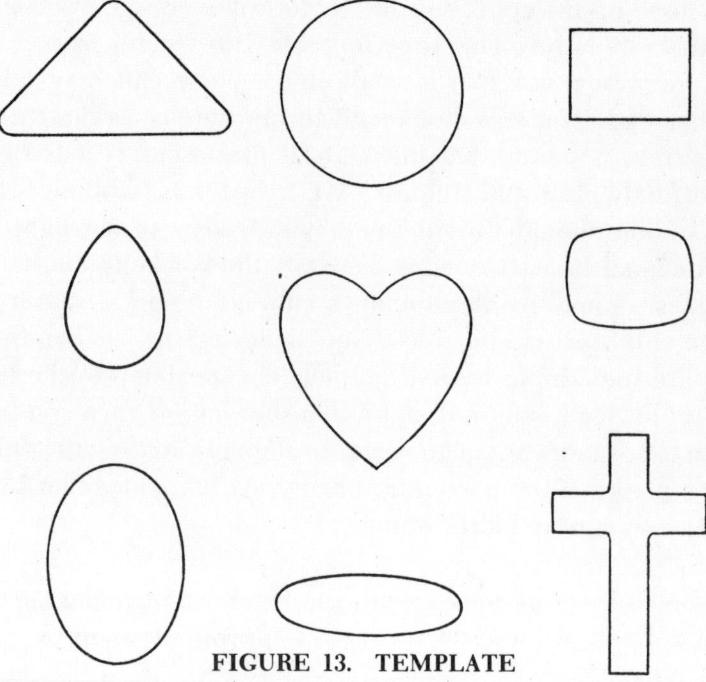

FIGURE 13. TEMPLATE

sometimes to the stone. Consequently, a lubricant is essential. The majority of lapidaries use a solution made up of four parts of kerosene to one part of light grade motor oil. I have often used kerosene without the motor oil and it has given good results.

The thin plastic sheet that is placed over a slice of rock (slab) to help determine the most advantageous size and shape the final stone should have is called a template. The sizes of the various forms are standard so that stones cut to these dimensions will fit standard findings. A *finding* is a piece of metal which may be purchased to hold the stone such as an earring, a cuff link or a brooch. Of course, if conformation to a standard finding would do violence to a beautiful section of the stone we prefer to keep that beauty and either fashion our own finding or ask a jeweler to create one.

There is no limit to the shapes that are possible; round, oval, teardrop, heart shaped, square, rectangular, octagonal or uneven. (See Figure 13.) The decision on shape ought to be determined by two principles: (*a*) a long enough look to achieve a composition that is pleasing (there are no set rules for composing a picture on canvas nor in centering objects in stone) and (*b*) the effort not to destroy other pictures on the stone. Another consideration is the utility of the stone for the particular purpose in mind. One can often use a particular moss agate for cuff links that would be too small and insignificant in a brooch. If one is simply developing a gallery of "pictures in stone" that will be mounted on various sizes of miniature easels, one has a great deal more latitude than if one is designing personal adornments. Some scenes in agate, in sandstone, in jasper are so integrated that it is little short of criminal to cut them for smaller uses. There are always stones that can be used for those purposes. In a sense we are saying that the slab itself ought to determine the form of presentation and not vice versa. I have often silently watched one or another of my friends hack up a beautiful simulated floral display in plume agate that was breathtaking as a scene in order to fit a small part in some piece of jewelry—but it was their stone, not mine.

The trim saw is a thinner and smaller saw. Its general purpose is to form the stone as closely as possible to the final shape desired. It, too, must be lubricated. Water or soluble oil is generally recommended. The trim saw makes only straight cuts and trying to make curves may damage the saw blade. Because the blade is thin, however, cuts across corners can be made so that the result of trimming is a shape quite close to the desired outline. Always allow sufficient material beyond the marked lines so that necessary grinding does not make the final stone too small.

Grinding

After the trim saw operation, the stone is put into final shape by grinding off corners or saw marks and forming the final shape of the piece. The name for stones cut and ground in this manner is *cabochon*.

The tools used for grinding purposes are circular, thick disks of abrasive minerals. The one commonly in use is silicon carbide. These wheels come with different sizes of mineral particles. (They come in various dimensions but the wheels that are 8 to 10 inches in diameter and 1 inch thick are very convenient.) The first grinding is performed on an abrasive with relatively large particles.

A first grinding uses a No. 60 grit. This grinding will rather quickly form the stone but because of the size of particles it will leave numerous scratches. These must be worked out on a second grinding wheel charged with smaller grit, generally a No. 180 grit. Both wheels turn at a speed of about 5,000 surface feet per minute although some lapidaries prefer a slower speed.

The stones are run at high speeds and again lubrication, this time with water, is most essential. Some lapidary units come with a ready-made water system that feeds a consistent amount of water on the wheel. Others are equipped with a pan and the wheel runs in the water. Good results come from squeezing a large sponge underneath the wheel so that the wheel runs on the sponge and the sponge lies in water which does not touch the wheel. The friction of the stone on the wheel is enormous and if the wheel runs dry, the friction causes such heat that many stones crack and fracture.

There are two ways that a stone can be applied to the grinding and sanding wheels. The stone can be held in the fingers or it can be cemented onto a dop stick. Figure 14 shows a stone correctly positioned on a dop stick. Note that the stone rests on the end of the stick, so that it is fully supported. The cement fully covers the base surface of the stone for maximum support, but does not extend beyond it, where it might interfere with the grinding process. Larger stones are generally held in the fingers because they can be held securely without injuring the fingers. This is very difficult with ½-inch stones, however. Hence the dop stick. The dop stick is a hardwood dowel about 6 inches long and ¼- to ½-inch in diameter. The diameter used depends on the size of the stone. The stone is cemented to the end of this stick by use of a special hard wax. This wax comes in small rectangular bars easily obtainable at any rock shop. A Bunsen or gas

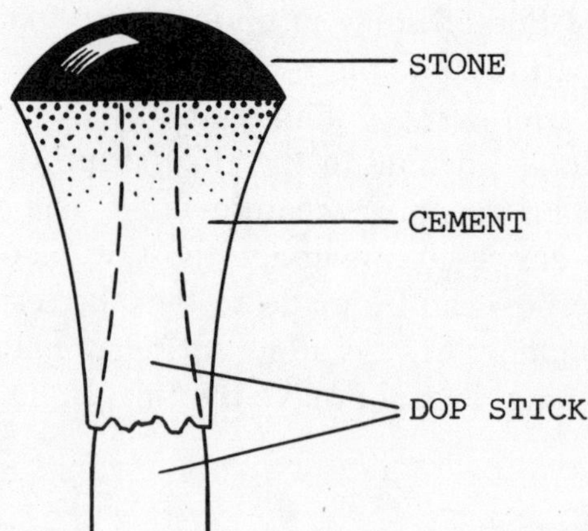

FIGURE 14.
PROPERLY CEMENTED STONE

flame is necessary to warm the stone and melt the wax. Both the stone and the bar of wax are passed through the flame of the Bunsen burner. Too great heat may damage both stone and wax. One hundred degrees or a little more is sufficient. The wax is put on the stick and rolled against a flat surface. This coats the top of the stick and extends some of the wax along the sides of the stick. The warm stone is now pressed firmly into the wax. The wax cools rapidly and can be formed about the base of the stone. When the stone has cooled the work of grinding begins.

Cabochon Fabrication

The basic characteristic of a cabochon is that it is domed on the viewing side while the back is flat. In cutting transparent stones, however, both the front and the back are domed so that the light passing through the front will be reflected. The edge of the finished stone, whether it is cabochoned or faceted, is called the girdle. It may have a sharp edge, a grooved edge, or a rounded edge, depending on the plan for setting or showing the finished "cab." If it is to be attached to a piece of jewelry by a wire, then a groove is required.

When as much material as possible has been cut away by the trim saw the stone will have a great many small angles and flat places. It must then be rotated slowly while held against the grinding wheel to attain the shape marked on it from the template. Of course this is not true of rectangular or square designs.

After the first grinding produces the desired shape the next step is to cut the dome. The height of the dome varies with the use of the stone and the aesthetic judgment of the cutter. Stones in cuff links generally have a low dome, but stones for rings may well have a medium or high dome. In the case of agates which have inclusions, the proportions of the stone sometimes depend on the way in which it must be ground to bring out a clear picture. In the case of fire opal or agate the proportions may be determined by a dome height which brings out maximum fire. Perhaps it is not necessary to add that doing such grinding properly requires a considerable amount of experience. The novice would be well advised to practice on less valued stones at the beginning. The flat part of the stone, whether held by the fingers or on a dop stick, is rhythmically rotated from side to side against the grinding wheel until the desired dome is achieved. The stone should be inspected frequently to make sure that the right amount of material is being removed all about the stone. It must have a consistent curved surface, regardless of whether a low or high dome is the goal. In beginning this task it helps to have a model to follow. Cabochoned stones are not expensive. They come in all shapes so that the beginner can generally find one that is very much like what he would like to do. During inspections the unfinished cab can be compared with the finished one. If the cab is held by hand it is a simple matter to turn it over and finish the back. However, if it is on a dop stick it will have to be removed and recemented on the finished side before that can be done. The last step is to bevel the sharp edge to about a 45-degree angle as

FIGURE 15. BEVELED EDGE OF CABOCHON

shown in Figure 15. The reason for this is to prevent chipping and to provide an edge which can be secure in a finding.

After the grinding of the rough stone the next step is a second grinding on a wheel that has much finer grit. This is called "finish" grinding. It eliminates the coarse marks left on the stone and brings the stone even closer to the planned shape and depth.

Sanding and Polishing

The next operation is sanding. Sanding may be done by hand or with a sanding machine. The purpose of sanding is twofold. It eliminates the marks on the stone left by fine grinding and it begins the polishing operation. If the operation is performed by hand, the stone is rotated with a quick motion over an abrasive cloth. Or the abrasive cloth is mounted on a drum which is turned by an electric motor at a speed of about 500 r.p.m.'s. Hand sanding is the safest operation, but this takes a good deal of time if one is working with a fairly large slab or cabochon. The sanding cloth comes in rolls which are from 1 inch to 2 inches in diameter and are fitted to the drum. Grinding out the scratches left from the fine grinding can be done on sanding grit of No. 180 to No. 220 size. Final sanding may use the same size of grit if it is well worn down or a fresh grit cloth of much finer grain can be used.

A word should be said here regarding the safety aspects of using the grinding and sanding wheels. If the operator becomes too eager and impatient and presses too hard on his stone or keeps it too long on the wheel it will grow very hot, the cementing medium will soften, and the stone may fly off. As it flies off at great speed it may be reflected back into the hands or the face of the operator. For this reason great care should be used to ensure the proper cementing of the stone on the dop stick and the frequent inspections already recommended. Furthermore, good usage involving any power machine includes wearing safety glasses. They are a small investment for safety. Nor should it be forgotten that excessive heat may fracture or crack the stone with the result being that all work to this point is wasted.

The same rhythmic motion is used in sanding as in grinding. The stone is turned from side to side so that all the surface is sanded and smoothed. Sanding can be judged to be completed when inspection under a magnifying glass shows only very fine scratches and the stone has achieved a moderately glossy look. After that condition is reached further sanding is a waste of time.

After one is satisfied with the sanding operation one moves to polishing. But before this operation is initiated it is important to carefully wash the specimen. If careful cleaning is not done a piece of grit from the sanding cloth may be left on the stone and it will cut small gouges in the stone during the polishing operation. Actually the stone should be scrubbed rather vigorously to dislodge any grit that may have become embedded during the previous operations.

The final polishing after sanding is done on a leather-covered drum which may be mounted in either an upright or horizontal position. In either case the leather is covered with a polishing powder called tin oxide. This powder is mixed with water and applied to the leather. As the stone presses against the leather the polish is worked into the leather. The polish must be kept at the proper degree of moistness. If it is too dry the stone and the leather will become too hot; if it is too wet there will not be enough friction to accomplish the polishing action.

The polishing operation is rather simple. The stone is rotated on the dop stick and moved from side to side so that all surfaces have an equal opportunity for the contact which results in the polishing action. The stone is frequently inspected to see the degree of gloss being achieved and to check on the heat of the stone. This operation takes very little time. If the stone is free from blemishes and the polishing agent has the right consistency only a couple of minutes are required.

After a high gloss is achieved, the final operation consists of removing the stone from the dop stick. This may be done by heating the wax to loosen it, but it is preferable to chip the wax away and then give the stone a *gentle* blow that will cleanly separate it from the dop stick. The remaining wax on the stone can be removed by a knife or by immersion in alcohol. After the wax is removed, the stone is again carefully washed to get rid of all residual particles of polish. The stone is then ready to be mounted or to be displayed.

Tumbling

In the course of sawing up slabs of stone a great many residual pieces are left over. Many of these pieces are too small for further fabrication, but some of them are of moderate size and beauty. Furthermore, in the field a number of smaller specimens are normally collected that are not really sized or proportioned for cabochoning. Many rockhounds use a tumbling machine to grind and polish these specimens. It is also possible to do the final grinding and polishing operation on cabochons in a tumbler. The tumbler has the great advantage of grinding and polishing a large number of stones at the same time.

The tumbler is a machine of very simple design. It consists of a barrel that is mounted on a rotating shaft driven by a small motor. These barrels come in all sizes. The stones to be polished are placed inside the barrel with a mixture of water and grinding and polishing agents. The constant rotation of the barrel results in the grinding and polishing operation being carried out on the stones inside. A rough grit is introduced with the stones. A No. 60 to No. 100 grit can be used for this initial charge. The barrel should rotate at a speed of about 30 r.p.m.'s for maximum results. Tumbling is not a speedy process. Generally one or two weeks are required for this first operation, depending on the hardness and contour of the stones. When the first stage is over and the rough areas from the diamond saw or surface blemishes from the field are eliminated this rough grit is removed, the barrel and stones are carefully washed and a second grit of No. 300 size is introduced. This is run for another week or two and is replaced, after washing, by a third grit (No. 600) for even finer polishing. Some rockhounds introduce a fourth stage, using No. 1200 grit, which is run for the same length of time. Others proceed without this step to introduce tin oxide. At this stage I have found that the use of small leather chips about one-half inch in diameter seems to accelerate the polishing action. Another week or two is necessary before the stones achieve a high polish.

Stones which for one reason or another are poorly ground after the first two operations should be removed and saved for another try. Likewise, stones which are not polished well at the conclusion of the last run can be introduced during the next polishing procedure. For some reason there always seem to be a few stones which are neither ground nor polished to the same degree as the others. This may be due to a different degree of hardness or simply to chance, but they should be redone.

We have been discussing the tools used and the procedures employed to fashion beautiful stones from field specimens by the use of grading, sanding and polishing tools and agents. Every rockhound ought to master these techniques before moving on to the more difficult and expensive ways of treating stones. It is not the purpose of this book to deal extensively with other methods of fabricating gems. Other books describe in careful detail the methodology utilized in the more sophisticated treatment of gems. But the following brief descriptions will add to the vocabulary of the beginner and will give him incentive to move on when he has mastered the techniques of gathering and treating stones in the ways that are described in this book.

Faceting means literally "to cut planes on a small piece of gem material." The purpose of faceting is to highlight the brilliance and beauty of gems. This is done technically by maximizing the reflection of light. It requires specialized machinery and specialized knowledge of both the stone and the procedure. Generally only such highly prized gems as diamond, emerald, ruby, sapphire, tourmaline, topaz, and garnet are faceted, because only they have both the color and hardness to make faceting worthwhile. In any case it is a difficult task and will require some tutoring. The rockhound who wishes to broaden his operations to include faceting will do well to enroll in a class presented by a local gem club or by a continuing education department for his introduction to this field.

Stone Carving and Sculpture may be the final goal of the rockhound. Not everyone possesses the imagination or the skill demanded for these pursuits. Indeed, not many of the ten million rockhounds in this country have attempted this difficult art. Carving in marble with a chisel is difficult enough, but carving the much harder gem materials is even more of a challenge. A whole new range of tools and skills is essential. The amateur rockhound would do well to mature in all of his skills with tools before he embarks on carving.

The fabrication of gems from rough stones brings out their hidden beauty and their value. It does something more for the rockhound. It makes his rockhounding purposeful and rewarding. Whether he does it simply to exhibit or for gifts to friends or for profit matters little. The fact that he has added the skill of a gem maker to his ability to find specimens in the field adds another dimension of depth to his experience. There is still a third area of growth. That has to do with giving these fabricated gems a proper setting, and we turn to that development in the next chapter.

6. How Do You Prepare and Share Gems?

MAN IS A SOCIAL creature. There are some introverts who prefer the seclusion of their study or workshop to any human interaction but they are few. Most of us increase the joy we desire from activity, and particularly creative activity, if we can share the results with others who respond to our efforts. This chapter is concerned with certain ways to identify, exhibit, and provide splendid settings for our gems and crystals.

Labeling and Displaying

There are certain conventions that grow up in all human endeavors and rock-hounding is no exception. One of the conventions has to do with proper labeling and recording of pertinent information about gems. If we are going to use them as specimens, the viewer is curious as to what the specimen is and where it was found. It is often important for him to know when it was found—particularly if the exhibit moves him to plan a field trip to obtain some of the same material. Consequently, some plan for cataloging gems and minerals must be developed. It can be done alphabetically or by class of minerals, or by locality; but some system ought to be devised so that a stranger looking at a label or going through your collection knows whether a gem was found in Indiana or India. It does not matter particularly how you label your finds as long as you are familiar with them and can answer questions about them. To do this requires some personal discipline. We do not always get to process finds the day after or even the week after we return from a field trip. Often, if we have not already made some kind of identification as to exactly where the specimen was obtained, our memory may be faulty and we will fall back on generalizations about areas that are not exact. Minerals ought to be labeled in the field and, when cleaned or processed, identified as part of a general catalog. Only small identifying numerals or letters need to be put on the specimen itself if they clearly refer back to a general catalog. On the catalog card, the following information is minimal: the date the specimen was collected, its species and variety within the species, the locality where it was found, how it was acquired—purchased, dug, or what have you—and any special notation about the way it was prepared for exhibit. If it was heat-treated to change its color this information ought to be included. Then its location in the collection should be indicated. As one broadens one's collection, the specimens may be stored in any number of places such as garage, rock shop, bedroom, or the closet. In any case, it will save much hunting later if the cabinet location in the house is noted.

Not all crystals and minerals are kept, we hope, in closets. There are attractive ways to allow guests in the home or shop to see specimens that have some particular meaning to the collector. I have a large glass cabinet (like the ones that merchants use to exhibit merchandise) in the hall beside my front door. In that cabinet are the cherished specimens that are "bragging and conversation stones." One of the rocks is a piece of crystal salt with a water inclusion. The water bubble roams around in this million-year-old salt relic! This is not a rock that the Smithsonian would put on exhibit, but a friend owns the mine from which it came and it is cherished. Next to the rock salt are some pieces of garnet *in matrix* from Idaho, a very nice Yogo sapphire *in matrix*, some Australian precious opal *in matrix*, a crystal of tourmaline in quartz, and other stones. At the other end of the cabinet are some Indian artifacts like hones, scrapers, etc., that I found when gem hunting. It is not a display that would excite any distinguished mineralogist or win a prize at a rock show, but these items happen to have meaning for me and consequently I show them to friends and tell their story.

Ingenious methods of display abound in many rockhound homes. One collector had a special dining-room table built. The top was heavy glass with a table-sized shelf under the glass filled with his best specimens. Others have designed special and beautiful wood doors which open to reveal shelf after shelf of crystals and cut stones. In addition to the gems that are displayed openly, almost everyone has cabinets with deep drawers for large rocks and tabletop cabinets that are shallower for smaller gems. But stones or cabochon stones that break easily, like turquoise, are generally kept under glass in Riker mounts. These are tough cardboard boxes with thick cotton batting pressed against the glass on the top of the box. The cotton holds the gems securely in place and makes a nice background against which to view colored or brilliant stones. Cabbed moss agates can be exhibited on one-inch-thick plates of styrofoam. One simply arranges the stones attractively on the plate and then presses them into place. The plates hold the stones nicely and are light in weight when one wants to transport them somewhere.

Many collectors specialize in the pictures that can be identified in different types of wood, sandstone, plume agate or moss agate. Science has come to the rescue of these exhibitors and one can purchase silver or nickel easels of various sizes. The exhibits sit on these like a painting. Such easels make very attractive home decorations and are quite easy to set up for a show. They are relatively inexpensive. Some glass or silver stands are available to hold faceted gems. One word of caution is in order. Crystals, cabs and gems are dust collectors. When first processed, they are admirable, but if allowed to accumulate dust, much of their fire and luster will be hidden. All exhibits ought to be kept in dustproof containers of some sort if possible. If there are some specimens that display better on an open shelf, these ought to be periodically and carefully cleaned. A soft paint brush does very well with most of them.

Jewelry Making

Many rockhounds eventually discover they wish to explore the art of jewelry making as a means of displaying and using the stones they have found and prepared. For this reason, almost every rock shop will have available standardized rings, brooches, cuff links, caps, and mounts that do very well to enclose the gems that have been either cabbed or faceted. When one is dealing with an indifferent stone, it is perhaps wise not to waste too much time on its setting and here the use of a standard finding would be an efficient use of time. However, for an unusual stone, an unusual mounting brings out its uniqueness and its beauty. The added dimension to finding and cutting a very good gem is to create a special setting for it which not only calls attention to the gem but enhances its effectiveness as a gem.

Creating special settings that are unique in platinum, silver, bronze or gold requires some background, knowledge, experience. One must learn how to handle various metals, become acquainted with such tools as blowtorches, ovens and soldering irons. One has to learn to carve and design. The hardest part is to learn how to design. One can be a silversmith, but without good design the technical skill goes for naught. How does one learn the principles of good design? Styles in design change, but beyond style there are basic principles of form, balance, perspective and color harmony that hold for all artistic media. It is perhaps for this reason that the classic books on jewelry design devote a great deal of attention to examples of good design. One learns by doing, but one also learns by looking. The design of any piece of jewelry is very complex. The design has the purpose of enhancing the stone. Consequently, there is a special art to designing a setting for a gem that will in theme and form add something special to the gem.

FIGURE 16.
BRONZE AND GLASS SCULPTURE

ARTIST: AUDREY PETERSON

ARTIST: AUDREY PETERSON

FIGURE 17. SAPPHIRE RING

ARTIST: AUDREY PETERSON

FIGURE 18. RING USING BAROQUE PEARL

Figure 16 shows an organic form holding rough blocks of colored glass. The artist had been particularly impressed by the beauty of several large chunks of colored glass which she purchased. She wanted to mount them in such a way that the mounting would not only highlight the glass but say something about it. She chose this trunk and lifelike bronze form to set out the glass in such a way that it would communicate to others the beauty she saw in those pieces. The setting has a kind of elemental statement about it which does more than just hold the pieces of glass. In some way, the glass is now more than glass . . . it has been enhanced.

The next picture (Figure 17) is that of a sapphire. It is, incidentally, the chartreuse sapphire that I found at the end of two days' digging in a dip, as I have already described. The stone had a particular shape and much would have been lost if it had been brilliant cut. It was free-formed and the cut displayed follows roughly the shape of the gem when it was first screened. At the end of this rather long and pointed sapphire there rests a small ruby which came from the same mine. The combination of chartreuse and ruby red may seem a strange one, but in fact they complement each other. The sapphire is rather large and the ruby is very small, but this too proves to be exciting. The white gold setting is leaflike and fragile, which seems to add even more importance to the two stones.

The next illustration (Figure 18) shows a way of using a "baroque" pearl. A pearl is not a gemstone, but is generally considered with gemstones. Baroque pearls are simply pearls that are malformed into interesting shapes. Some of them are far more intriguing than a simple spherical pearl. In this case the pearl is set upon a long, silver prong. It is placed against a background of cast silver, but the silver background is to one side of the pearl. The technical reason for this is that the pearl, which is the focal point of this piece of sculpture, must be seen from all angles. Set high and in this setting, no one can miss the message of the artist that here is an object that demands attention. The silver also picks up some of the grey sheen of the pearl itself.

This book is not intended as a primer in jewelry making. What is required is some imagination, patience, and again a great deal of background knowledge, practice and technical skill. Not everyone will be motivated to move from gem collecting and processing to jewelry making. Not everyone should. But some examples have been illustrated here for those who may be intrigued with this aspect of the hobby. However, enough has been said to indicate that this is a very specialized pursuit and requires specialized training. Persons interested in jewelry making will want to read basic books about silver and gold fabrication, to be initiated in special classes, and to begin their work under the watchful eye of a good teacher.

Conclusion

It is possible and satisfying for a collector to assemble an array of crystals and minerals by buying them at rock shops and at rock shows. He will learn a great deal about his environment by doing this. For such a person, it will be more satisfying to go into the hills and valleys and collect his own specimens, and then clean, mount, and display them. Others will not be content with this level of achievement. These rockhounds will want to process their stones by learning how to cabochon and facet. They will find more satisfaction in having added their skill to processing the gemstones which nature provides. These rockhounds can display their gems at shows and give them to friends. For still others, this is not enough. They will wish to add their own touch of imagination to the setting by which a jewel is displayed in a case or on a finger. They will want to master the principles of design, metal processing and setting. For them, the final accolade will be the satisfaction of having discovered, dug, cut and set the jewel. The whole process is theirs and the inner satisfaction is complete. However, faceting, casting and forging require a considerable outlay of money and time. No one dictates at what level the rockhound must function. At every stage, the process is rewarding and creative.

APPENDIX

Where Gemstones Are Found

This list of gemstones and where they are to found in the United States had as its core the original listing prepared by Dorothy M. Schlegel for her *Gemstones of the United States.* A massive amount of work went into compiling that list, but now it is obviously out of date. The basic list was then compared with the authoritative work of J. Sinkankas in his *Gemstones of North America.* This is a monumental book rich in descriptions of gems, specific in terms of locations, and stimulating in its historical and geological explanations. The beginning rockhound cannot do better than to acquire and read this book. After adding material from Sinkankas the list was further compared with many regional lists and finally revised in terms of the author's own experience in the field. This list must be used with extreme caution, however. Many of the deposits described have no doubt been exhausted. Other areas have been closed. Consequently all the rules given earlier about checking locations apply. A few letters or phone calls can save one from taking many fruitless field trips.

State and County	*Locality*	*Gemstone*
ALABAMA		
Coosa	Rockford	gem beryl, corundum
	Hissop	corundum
Jefferson	Nobbs Property	turquoise
Marshall	Guntersville	quartz crystal
Tallapoosa	Zana	smoky quartz
ARIZONA		
Apache	Tanner Springs	wood
	Ganado	pyrope
	Navajo Reservation	peridot, pyrope
	Buel Park, Fort Defiance	pyrope, peridot
	Petrified Forest National Monument (no collecting)	wood
	Sanders	agate
	Concho	agate
Cochise		tourmaline
	Copper Queen mine, Bisbee	azurite, chrysocolla, malachite
	Turquoise Mountain	turquoise
	Courtland	turquoise, azurite
	Tombstone	turquoise
	Dragoon	chrysoprase, chrysocolla
Coconino		tourmaline, wood
	Willow Springs	wood
	Lees Ferry	wood
Gila	Castle Dome mine	turquoise
	Globe	chrysoprase
	Miami	chrysoprase
	Inspiration mine	chrysocolla, chalcedony
	Keystone mine	chrysocolla, chalcedony
	San Carlos	peridot
Graham		agate
	Graham Mountain	uvarovite, andradite
Greenlee	Morenci	azurite, garnet
	York	fire agate, carnelian, agate, jasper
	Metcalf	malachite
Maricopa		agate, tourmaline
	Aguila	chalcedony
	Gila Canyon	chrysoprase, grossularite
	Four Peaks	amethyst
	Morristown	turquoise
	Camp Creek	jasper
	Cavecreek	jasper

State and County	Locality	Gemstone
ARIZONA *(cont.)*		
Maricopa *(cont.)*		
	Skunk Creek	jasper
	Pierce	turquoise
	Wickenburg	carnelian
Mohave	Aquarius	chalcedony,
	Mountains, Owens	opal
	Black Mountains	chrysoprase
	Ithaca Peak and Aztec Mountain	chrysoprase, jasper, turquoise, azurite
	Mineral Park	turquoise
	Oatman	chalcedony, amethyst, opal
Navajo	Holbrook	amethyst, petrified wood
Pima		tourmaline, agate, garnet, jasper
Pinal	Kelvin	turquoise, tourmaline
	Saddle Mountain	agate
	Superior	obsidian, azurite
Yavapai		tourmaline, azurite, malachite, opal, agate, jasper
	Crystal Peak	quartz crystals
Yuma	Brenda	jasper
	Muggins Mountain	agate
ARKANSAS		
Garland	Jessieville	quartz crystal, malachite
Hot Spring	Magnet Cove	smoky quartz, quartz crystal, sunstone, topazolite, garnet
	near Morrison	jasper
Madison	Delaney	quartz crystal
Montgomery	Crystal Mountain	quartz crystal
Pike	Murfreesboro	diamond
	Paron	quartz crystal
CALIFORNIA		
Alameda	Berkeley	agate thunder eggs
	Livermore	quartz, citrine
	Newman Mine	citrine
Alpine	Hope Valley, Mogul, Monitor districts	rose quartz
Amador	Indian Gulch	diamond
	Shake Ridge, Volcano	amethyst, rose quartz, smoky quartz, diamond, amethyst

State and County	*Locality*	*Gemstone*
CALIFORNIA *(cont.)*		
Amador *(cont.)*	Ione	chrysoprase
	Sutter Creek	black gold quartz
Butte		gold quartz
	Cherokee Flats	diamond
	Big Bar, Yankee Hill, and Oroville	grossularite
	Pulga	idocrase (californite)
	Feather River	smoky quartz
Calaveras	Garnet Hill	andradite
	Green Mountain mine, Chile Gulch, Mokelumne Hill	quartz crystal
	Murphys	jasper
	Sheepranch Mine	black gold quartz
Del Norte	Smith River	diamond, jasper
	Crescent City	agate, jasper, wood
El Dorado		gold quartz, rock crystals
	Placerville	smoky quartz, diamond
	Webber Hill	diamond
	Traverse Creek	californite
Fresno	Taylor's Ranch, Chowchilla River	turquoise
	Jacolito Canyon	orbicular chert
Humboldt	French lode, Eureka district	cat's eye, prase
	Imperial Black Hills	agate, amethyst
Inyo	San Carlos Mine	chalcedony, essonite, lapis lazuli, opal
Kern		rose quartz, garnet, wood
	Saltdale	fire opal
	Horse Canyon	agate
Los Angeles	Howard Springs	amethyst
	Acton	jasper
Marin		nephrite
	Sausalito	jasper
Mariposa		gold quartz
Modoc		labradorite, jasper, agate
	Cape San Martin area	nephrite
	Jade Cove, Jenny Creek	carnelian
	Sailor Flat Mining Camp	opalized wood
Monterey		nephrite, jasper
Nevada	French Corral	diamond
Placer		gold quartz
	Green Valley, American River	uvarovite
Plumas	Gopher Hill	diamond
	Laura quartz mine, Clio	opal

State and County	*Locality*	*Gemstone*
CALIFORNIA *(cont.)*		
Plumas *(cont.)*	Peters Mine	rhodonite
	Meadow Valley	jasper, rose quartz
	Spanish Creek	diamond
Riverside	Coahuila Mountain	green and golden beryl, kunzite, smoky quartz, quartz crystal, rose quartz, tourmaline
	Mule Mountains	fire agate
	Crestmore	garnet
	Hemet	essonite, morganite, rose quartz, topaz, tourmaline
San Benito	Clear Creek	jadeite, uvarovite, quartz
San Bernardino		jasper, topaz, agate
	Barstow	opal, sapphire, agate, jasper, wood, palm root
	Manuel District	turquoise
	Upland	lapis lazuli
	Brown Mountain	bloodstone
	Calico Mountains	quartz, wood, agate
	Cascade Canyon	lapis lazuli
	near Baker	turquoise
	Cottonwood Station	turquoise
	Death Valley	bloodstone
	Newberry	fire opal, jasper
	Opal Mountain	precious opal
	San Bernardino Mountains	agate
	Nipton	turquoise
	Victor	turquoise
San Diego		aquamarine, essonite, kunzite, jasper, golden and green beryl, morganite, rose quartz, quartz crystal, tourmaline, topaz, spessartite
	Emeratite No. 2 Mine	topaz
	Hiriat Hill	spodumene
	Dos Cabezas Springs	essonite
	Mesa Grande district	rose quartz, tourmaline, beryl, garnet
	Pala district	golden beryl, rose quartz, kunzite, tourmaline
	Good Hope mine	grossularite
	Ramona	aquamarine, rose quartz, tourmaline, topaz, spessartite
	Rincon	tourmaline, kunzite, beryl
San Francisco	Land's End Station	jasper
Santa Barbara	Santa Barbara	quartz crystal
Santa Clara	Morgan Hill	jasper (flowering jasper)
Shasta	Hart	jasper (flowering jasper)

State and County	*Locality*	*Gemstone*
CALIFORNIA *(cont.)*		
Sierra		gold quartz
Siskiyou	Dunsmuir	garnet, opal
	Jenne Creek, Hornbrook	sard, carnelian
	Chan Jade mine	idocrase, jade
	Happy Camp	idocrase
	Wheeler Prospect	rhodonite
Sonoma	Cloverdale *and* Valley Ford	jadeite
	Petaluma	wood, jasper
	Glen Ellen	fire opal
Trinity	North Fork of the Eel River	jadeite, nephrite
	Carrvillo	garnet, green
	Trinity River	diamond
Tulare		nephrite
	Alpine Creek	diamond
	Lemoncove	rose quartz, rhodonite
	Lindsay	californite
	Porterville	chrysoprase
	Rattlesnake	pyrope
	Lemoncove district	rhodonite
	Tobias Mountain, Exeter, Yokohol	rose quartz
	Venice Hill, Visalia	chrysoprase
Tuolumne	Lindsay	gold quartz, chrysoprase
	Jacksonville	uvarovite
Yuba		gold quartz
COLORADO		
Alamosa	King Mine, San Louis Valley	turquoise
Arapahoe	Deer Trail	amazonite
Boulder		chrysoberyl, beryl
Chaffee	Calumet Iron Mine, Turret	essonite, quartz crystal, sapphire, sagenite
	Calumet Mine, Salida	ruby
	Chalk Creek, Buena Vista	sapphire
	Dorothy Hill	quartz crystal, almandite
	Mt. Antero	aquamarine, quartz, phenakite
	Ruby Mountain area, Nathrop	spessartite, topaz
	Nathrop	topaz, garnet
	White Mountain	aquamarine, quartz
Clear Creek	Red Elephant Mountain, Lawson	amethyst
	Silver and Trail Creeks, Idaho Springs	amethyst
Conejos	King Turquoise Mine, Manassa	turquoise
Custer		amazonite

State and County	*Locality*	*Gemstone*
COLORADO *(cont.)*		
Douglas	Devils Head	amazonite, smoky quartz, topaz
	Larkspur	jasper
	Pine Creek Store near Sedalia	quartz crystal, amazonite, smoky quartz
El Paso		petrified wood
	Austin Bluffs, Colorado Springs	carnelian, jasper
	Cheyenne Canyon	topaz
	Pikes Peak area	amethyst, tourmaline, topaz
	Manitou Springs	smoky quartz
	St. Peter's Dome	amazonite, quartz crystal, smoky quartz, topaz
	near Calumet	sapphire
	Canon City	almandite, amethyst, opal, rose quartz, corundum, tourmaline
	Chalk Mountain, Fremont Pass	spessartite, topaz, smoky quartz
	Curio Hill	agate
	Felch Creek	agate, jasper, geodes
	Wet Mountains, Garden Park near Canon City	jasperized bones, agate
	Parkdale	aquamarine
	Royal Gorge	aquamarine, tourmaline
	Texas Creek	rose quartz, gem beryl
Garfield		chrysoprase
Gilpin	Central City	labradorite, moss agate
Grand	Willow Creek, Hot Sulphur Springs	agate, chrysoprase
Gunnison	Italian Mountain, Crested Butte	lapis lazuli
	Quartz Creek	tourmaline, beryl, lepidolite
	Mount Beckwith	moonstone
Jefferson	Centennial Cone, Golden	gem beryl, smoky quartz
	Drew Hill Golden	chrysoberyl
Lake	Turquoise Chief mine, St. Kevin mining district, Leadville	turquoise
Larimer	Pennoyer amethyst mine, Red Feather Lakes, Fort Collins	amethyst, rose quartz
	Specimen Mountain, Rocky Mountain National Park	agate, geodes, onyx, opal
Mesa	Glade Park Opal Hill, Fruita	opalized wood
	Pinon mesa	banded and moss agate, chalcedony
	Grand Junction	carnelian
Mineral	Amethyst mine, Bachelor Mountain, Creede	amethyst
	Commodore Mine, Eunice Mine, P. & E. Mine, Happy Thought	amethyst

State and County	*Locality*	*Gemstone*
COLORADO *(cont.)*		
Mineral *(cont.)*	Mine	
	West Willow Creek, North Creede	amethyst, turquoise matrix
	Wolf Creek Pass, San Juan Mountains	agate, moonstone
Montrose	near Uncompahgre	heliotrope
Ouray	Mount Sneffels	andradite, topazolite, amethyst
Park	Agate Plateau, Guffey	agate
	Mount Antero summit	smoky quartz
	Old Salt Works, Antero Junction	chalcedony, bloodstone, moss agate
	South Park, near Grand River	almandite, heliotrope
	Hartsell	agate, jasper, wood
	Tarryall Mountains	amazonite, smoky quartz, topaz
Pitkin	Roaring Fork, near Clear Creek and Bear Creek	rose quartz
Rio Grande	Del Norte	plume agate, chalcedony, opal, quartz crystal
Saguache	Hall Turquoise mine, Villa Grove	turquoise
	La Garita Creek	agate
San Juan	Silverton	amethyst
Teller	Cripple Creek area	amethyst
	Crystal Peak, Florissant	amethyst, quartz crystal, smoky quartz, geodes, sagenite, amazonite, topaz, garnet, rutilated quartz
	Crystal Park	amazonite, smoky quartz, topaz
	Stove Mountain	amazonite, smoky quartz, topaz
Weld	Kalouse	jasper, agate, wood, bone
CONNECTICUT		
Fairfield	Bethel	tourmaline
	Branchville	kunzite, apatite, beryl quartz
	Monroe	tourmaline
	Trumbull Township	topaz, quartz, tourmaline
Lincoln	Graves Mountain	kyanite, lazulite, rotile
Litchfield		aquamarine, gold beryl, staurolite, garnet
Middlesex	Haddam	aquamarine, chrysoberyl, spessartite, tourmaline
	Strickland Quarry	tourmaline, spodumene, smoky quartz
	Portland	aquamarine, tourmaline
New Haven	New Haven	andradite
	Southbury	rose quartz

State and County	Locality	Gemstone
CONNECTICUT (cont.)		
New London	New London	apatite
Windham	Willimantic	topaz, beryl
	Oneco	apatite
FLORIDA		
Hillsborough		fossil coral, chalcedony, coral geodes
Pinella	Tampa Bay, Tarpon Springs	fossil coral
GEORGIA		
Bulloch		fire opal
Chatham		heliotrope, jasper
Cherokee	Canton	almandine
Clay		diamond
Clayton	Morrow Station	diamond
Fannin		malachite
Floyd	Rome	quartz crystal
Franklin		quartz crystal
Hall	Gainesville	diamond
Morgan	Buckhead	amethyst
Paulding	Little Bob Copper mine	almandine
Pickens	Cook Farm	beryl
Rabun	Laurel Creek mine	ruby, sapphire
	Ledbetter mine, Clayton and Highland	amethyst, aquamarine, golden beryl, quartz crystal
Towns	Old Garrett mine, Charlie Creek	amethyst
Troup	Mineral Processing Company	rose quartz, beryl
Union	Hightower Bald	amethyst
Upson	Herron Mine	beryl
	Wilmot's Revine	agate
Washington		fire opal
IDAHO		
Adams	Rock Flat gold placer, near New Meadows	sapphire, diamond, garnet, topaz
Bear Lake	Paris Canyon, Humming Bird mine	jasper, quartz
Benewah	Alder Creek, Fernwood	chrysocolla, garnet

State and County	Locality	Gemstone
IDAHO (cont.)		
Blaine	Little Wood River	azurite, amethyst, jasper
Boise		topaz
	Centerville	aquamarine
	Deadwood Gulch	pyrope, spessartite
Canyon	Graveyard Point	plume agate
	Snake River	common opal
Clearwater	Pierce, along Rhodes and Orofino Creeks	sapphire, garnet
Custer		azurite
	Pole Creek	amethyst
	Resort	corundum
	Salmon River	agate, jasper
	American River	zircon
Fremont	Crystal Butte	andesine
	Homewood	agate
Latah		common opal, beryl, precious opal
Lemhi	Panther Creek	common opal, beryl, precious opal
Lincoln	Clover Creek	opalized wood
Nez Perce	Lewiston	almandite, aquamarine
	Silcott	precious opal
Oneida	Blackstone mine	azurite
Owyhee	Squaw Creek	common opal, precious opal
Shoshone	Mullan, Hunter	azurite
Washington		gem corundum, sapphire
	Fourth of July Canyon	opalized wood
	Goose Creek	agate
	Seven Devils district	chryscolla
	Weiser Cove	agate
ILLINOIS		
Alexander	Fayville	jasper
Hancock	Hamilton, Warsaw	quartz, agate, jasper
Hardin	Rosiclare	fluorite
Henry	Bishop Hill	agate
INDIANA		
Brown	Lick Creek	diamond, corundum
	Trevlac	geodes
Marion	Indianapolis	amethyst, moonstone
Morgan		bronze-colored sapphire, zircon, garnet
	Martinsville	diamond

State and County	*Locality*	*Gemstone*
IOWA		
Dubuque	Dubuque	agate, wood
Des Moines		quartz crystal
Henry	Mount Pleasant	agate, flint, quartz
Lee	Keokuk	geodes
Story	Ames	chalcedony
Van Buren	Farmington	geodes
KANSAS		
Barber	Ames	agate
Logan	El Rader	agate
McPherson	Marquette	quartz
Marshall	Platte River	agate, moss opal
Riley	Stockdale	pyrope
Trego	Collyer	jasper
Wallace	Wallace	opal
KENTUCKY		
Elliott		diamond
	Sandy Hook, Ison Creek	pyrope
Jefferson	Louisville	agate
Russell	Cabin Fork Creek	diamond
LOUISIANA		
Livingston Parish	Amite River	wood, jasper, carnelian
Ouachita Parish	Ouachita River	wood, jasper, carnelian
Vernon Parish	Leesville	palm wood
MAINE		
Androscoggin	Auburn	golden beryl, smoky quartz, tourmaline
	Minot	smoky quartz, topaz, tourmaline
	Mount Apatite, Littlefield Farm	apatite, smoky quartz, tourmaline, aquamarine, golden beryl
	Poland	golden beryl, tourmaline
	Windham Center	staurolite
Cumberland	Diamond Island, Portland	quartz crystal
	Harbor, Brunswick	beryl
Hancock	Mount Desert	amazonite
Kennebec	Windsor	aquamarine

State and County	*Locality*	*Gemstone*
MAINE *(cont.)*		
Oxford		essonite
	Albany	golden beryl, rose quartz, tourmaline
	Andover	essonite, hiddenite, kunzite
	Bethel	aquamarine, garnet
	Buckfield	milky quartz crystals, aquamarine, tourmaline
	Denmark	milky quartz crystals, aquamarine, tourmaline, amethyst
	French Mountain	aquamarine
	Grafton	aquamarine
	Greenwood Mountain	aquamarine, tourmaline, morganite
	Hebron	tourmaline, beryl, garnet
	Lovell	aquamarine
	Mount Mica, Paris	amazonite, rose quartz crystals, tourmalinated quartz, sagenite, aquamarine, tourmaline, morganite
	Mount Pleasant	smoky quartz, amethyst
	Newry Township	rose quartz crystals, aquamarine, tourmaline
	Norway Township	aquamarine, rose quartz, tourmaline
	Peru, Speckled Mountain	golden beryl
	Ragged Jack Mountain	chrysoberyl
	Rumford Falls	tourmaline, topaz
	Black Mountain Mica mine	spodumene
	Nevel Quarry Pit	spodumene
	Stoneham Lord's Hill	aquamarine, golden beryl, smoky quartz, topaz
	Stow	amethyst
Sagadahoc	Phippsburg	essonite, aquamarine, golden beryl
	Topsham	aquamarine, tourmaline, topaz
	Edececomo Mountain	beryl
MARYLAND		
Baltimore	Arundel gneiss quarry, Gunpowder River	aquamarine
	Bare Hills	moss agate, malachite
	Granite	amethyst
Carroll	between Middleburg and Big Pipe Creek	chrysocolla
Harford	Fliatville	agate, jasper
Howard	Davis	pyrope, quartz
Montgomery	Kensington mica mine, Burnt Mills	golden beryl
	Rockville Quarry	idocrase
Prince Georges	Beltsville	wood

State and County	*Locality*	*Gemstone*
MASSACHUSETTS		
Essex	Gloucester	quartz
	Rowley	jasper
Franklin	Northfield	aquamarine, golden beryl, garnet
	Deerfield	agate
Hampden	Blandford	aquamarine, golden beryl
Hampshire	Chesterfield	emerald, tourmaline, staurolite
	Lithia	spodumene
	Goshen	aquamarine, emerald, smoky quartz, tourmaline
	Cummington	rhodonite
	Norwich	aquamarine, golden beryl
Middlesex	Boxborough	apatite, garnet
Worcester	Berkshire Hills	jasper
	Fitchburg	aquamarine
	Royalston	aquamarine, golden beryl
	Bolton	apatite
	Sterling	spodumene
MICHIGAN	Lake Superior region	agate
Berrien	Buchanan	diamond
Cass	Dowagiac	diamond
Houghton	Houghton	chrysocolla, epidote, agate, thomsonite
Kent	Grand Rapids	rose quartz
Keweenaw	Keweenaw Penninsula, at Thunder Bay Allouez mine	amethyst, agate, thomsonite, chrysocolla, chalcedony, jasper (jaspillite)
Mackinac	Raber	calcified corals
MINNESOTA	Gunflint Lake	agate
Cook	Beaver Bay	agate
	Cascade	thomsonite
	Crow Ironton	crystalline quartz
	Grand Marais	agate
	Tofte	agate
Goodhue	Goodhue	quartz
Lake	Little Marais	agate
Morrison	Royalton	staurolite
MISSISSIPPI		
Copiah	Wesson	agate
Harrison	Bell Creek	agate

State and County	*Locality*	*Gemstone*
MISSOURI		
Clark	Kahoka	quartz
Crawford		azurite
Dent		azurite
Iron	Iron Mountain	smoky quartz
Lewis	La Grange	Lake Superior agate
Phelps		azurite
Washington	Potosi	agate, quartz
MONTANA		
Beaverhead	Frying Pan Basin	wood
Chouteau	Northeastern part	sapphire
Dawson	Glendive, Yellowstone River 100 miles to Billings	moss agate
Deer Lodge	Cable mine	chrysocolla
	Dry Cottonwood Creek	sapphire
Gallatin	Bozeman	corundum, topaz
	Mt. Blackmore	opal
	Yellowstone, Madison, Gallatin Rivers	wood
Glacier	Nelson Hill, near Blackfoot	diamond
Granite	Philipsburg	chrysocolla, sapphire
	Quartz Gulch	sapphire
	Rock Creek	sapphire
Jefferson	Homestake mining district, Butte	amethyst, smoky quartz
Judith Basin	Yogo	sapphire, ruby
Lewis and Clark	Helena	sapphire, ruby, garnet
	Canyon Ferry, Missouri River	sapphire, ruby, garnet
	Eldorado Bar	sapphire, ruby, garnet
	Three Mile Gulch	smoky quartz
Madison	Alder, Ruby River	garnet, onyx
	Pole Creek	sapphire
Silver Bow	East Ridge	chrysocolla
	Foothills, Butte district	rhodonite
	Browns Gulch	sapphire
Sweet Grass	Big Timber	agate

State and County	*Locality*	*Gemstone*
NEBRASKA		
Dawes		moss agate, chalcedony
Deuel	Chappell	agate, jasper, wood
Douglas		moss agate, chalcedony
Keith		moss agate, chalcedony
Morrill	Angora	moss opal
Scotts Bluff		moss agate, chalcedony
Sioux		moss agate, chalcedony
	Orella	agate
NEVADA		
Churchill	Sunnyside district	malachite
	Battle Mountain	wood, agate, jasper
Clark	Black Canyon, Colorado River	almandite
	Bullion district	chrysocolla, malachite
	Boulder City	agate, jasper, obsidian
	Crescent	turquoise
	Henderson	turquoise, jasper
	Las Vegas	azurite
	Searchlight	gold quartz, turquoise
Elko	Carlin	rose quartz
	Mountain City	azurite
	Tuscarora	citrine, rose quartz, agate
Esmeralda	Blair Junction	turquoise
	Coal Dale	turquoise, opalized wood
	Candelaria Mountains	variscite
	Cuprite district	malachite
	Gold Mountain	citrine
	Millers	turquoise
	Monte Cristo Mountains	variscite
	Palmetto Canyon	citrine
	Silver Peak Mountains	rose quartz
Eureka	Ruby Hill and Eureka district, Beowawe	azurite, turquoise
Humboldt	Coyote Springs	agate
	Virgin Valley	agate, precious opal
Lander	Austin	opal, rhodochrosite
	Battle Mountain	turquoise
Lyon	Yerington	turquoise
Mineral	Sodaville	turquoise, variscite
Nye	Beatty	agate modules, wood
	Belmont	petrified wood, turquoise
	Cactus Mountain, Butler	turquoise

State and County	*Locality*	*Gemstone*
NEVADA *(cont.)*		
Pershing	Duckwater	agate
	Tonopah	black jade, turquoise
	Lincoln Hill	quartz
	Pahute Mesa	agate
Washoe	Reno	turquoise
White Pine	Nightingale district, near Lane City	almandite
NEW HAMPSHIRE		
Belknap	Gilmanton	jasper
Carroll	Chatham, South Bald Face Mountain	beryl, topaz
	Love Joy Gravel Pits	topaz
	Mount Kearsarge	amethyst, rose quartz
Cheshire	Hinsdale	indicolite
	Keene	rose quartz
	Sullivan, Nims mica mine	aquamarine, golden beryl
	Surry	amethyst
	Walpole	indicolite
	Westmoreland	amethyst
	Winchester	indicolite
Coos	Berlin	amethyst
	Green Ledges	smoky quartz, topaz, amethyst
	Diamond Ledges	smoky quartz, topaz, amethyst
	Jasper Cave	jasper
	Victor's Head	topaz
	Stark	amethyst, quartz
	White Mountains, Mount Washington	rose quartz
	Milan	amethyst, smoky quartz, topaz
Grafton	Franconia	andradite, azurite, green rock crystal
	Grafton	almandite, topaz, aquamarine, golden beryl, smoky quartz
	Hanover	almandite, jasper, quartz crystal, rutilated quartz
	Orange	aquamarine, chrysoberyl
	Warren	essonite
Hillsboro	Amherst	essonite
	Francestown	jasper
Merrimack	Danbury, P.K. Filbert Farm	almandite, golden beryl
Strafford	Center Strafford	aquamarine, golden beryl
Sullivan		golden beryl
	Acworth, Beryl Mountain	almandite, aquamarine, rose quartz, golden beryl
	Springfield	spessartite

State and County	Locality	Gemstone
NEW JERSEY		
Cape May	Cape May	quartz crystal, jasper
	Belleville and Bloomfield	malachite
Hudson	Hoboken	agate, amethyst, black quartz
	Arlington	azurite, malachite, chrysocolla
Middlesex	South Amboy, South River	amber, agate, opal
Monmouth	Long Branch	quartz crystal
Morris	Alan Wood Iron mine	sunstone
Passaic	Hawthorne	agate
	Paterson	amethyst, agate, jasper
	Prospect Park	opal, agate
	Great Notch	agate
Somerset	Bound Brook	agate, amethyst, jasper, chrysocolla
	Lyons Station	amethyst geodes
	Somerville	turquoise
Sussex	Franklin	amethyst, beryl, sapphire, rhodonite, cyprine
	Furnace	quartz
	Andover	garnet
	Edison	feldspar, sunstone, ruby
NEW MEXICO		
Catron	Mogollon district	jasper
Colfax	Elizabeth Town	chrysocolla, garnet, malachite
Dona Ana	Organ, Torpedo mine	chrysocolla, quartz
Grant	Black Range, Great Republic mine	amethyst, moonstone
	Burro Mountains, Porterfield mines	chrysocolla, turquoise
	Fort Bayard	opal
	Little Hachita Mountains	turquoise, malachite, garnet
	Santa Rita	fire opal
	Silver City	essonite, agate, turquoise
	White Signal district	turquoise
Lincoln	Ancho	jasper
	Nogal	turquoise
Luna	Deming	agate
	Fremont	azurite, malachite
McKinley	Fort Wingate	peridot
Mora	Coyote	malachite
Otero	Jarilla	chrysocolla, turquoise, malachite, tourmaline

State and County	*Locality*	*Gemstone*
NEW MEXICO *(cont.)*		
Rio Arriba	Bromide	azurite, malachite, amazonite
	Canary Bird Mine	aquamarine
	Sunnyside Mine	
San Juan		jasper
	Navajo and Zuni Reservations	pyrope
San Miguel	Jemes	feldspar, labradorite
	Las Vegas	wood
	Tecolote	azurite, malachite
Sandoval	Cochiti district	opal
	Jemez Sulphur district	opal, jasper
	Nacimiento	chrysocolla, azurite, malachite, agate
Santa Fe		sapphire, wood, beryl, peridot
	Cerrillos	turquoise
Sierra	Caballo	malachite
	Kingston district	rhodonite
	Jornado Valley	jasper, agate, wood
	Truth or Consequences	wood
Socorro	Oscura Mountains	chrysocolla, azurite, malachite
	Jesepa	jasper, agate, quartz
	Fragristobal Range	opal
Taos		pyrope, andalusite, beryl, chrysocolla, garnet, apatite, rhodochrosite
Valencia	Copperton, Zuni Mountains	malachite
NEW YORK		
Albany		heliotrope
Essex		almandite, tourmaline, labradorite
	Crown Point	sunstone
Herkimer		quartz crystal, smoky quartz, rock crystal
	Diamond Hill, Salisbury	quartz crystal
	Little Falls	quartz crystal
	Middleville	quartz crystal
	Newport	quartz crystal
Lewis	Essex	labradorite
	Manhattan borough	aquamarine
Ontario	Geneva	smoky quartz
Orange	Blooming Grove, along Hudson River, Amity	heliotrope, jasper
Otsego	Toddsville	sapphire
Putnam	Tilly Foster mine, Brewster, Pine Island	grossularite, uvarovite
Richmond	Staten Island	prase

State and County	*Locality*	*Gemstone*
NEW YORK *(cont.)*		
St. Lawrence	De Kalb	chrysoprase, tourmaline
	Gouverneur	tourmaline, apatite
	Massena	diamond
	Pierrepont	tourmaline
Saratoga	Greenfield	chrysoberyl
	Overlook	rose quartz
Warren	Gore Mountain, North Creek	almandite
	Ruby Mountain	almandine
	Oven Mountain	almandine
	Lake George	quartz crystal, smoky quartz
	Riparius	garnet
Westchester	Bedford Village	asteriated quartz, golden beryl, rose quartz
	Bayless Quarry	rose quartz
	Chappaqua	sunstone
	Kinkel and Hobby quarries, North Castle	golden beryl, rose quartz
NORTH CAROLINA		
Alexander		pyrope
	Barrett Mountain	aquamarine
	Emerald-Hiddenite mine	emerald
	Hiddenite	rutilated quartz, aquamarine
	Stony Point	amethyst, citrine, emerald, golden beryl, hiddenite, quartz crystal, tourmalinated quartz, smoky quartz
	Taylorsville	citrine, smoky quartz, beryl
Ashe		rose quartz, feldspar
	Phoenix Mountain, Long Shoals Creek, Chestnut Hill Township	quartz crystal
	Allegheny Bald Knob	rhodonite
Avery		almandite
	Linville	chalcedony
Buncombe	Asheville	aquamarine
Burke		citrine, almandite, quartz crystal, rutilated quartz, smoky quartz, beryl
	Brindletown Creek Ford	diamond
	Burkemont, South Mountains	gem beryl
	Morganton, Laurel Creek	pyrope
	South Mountains, Joel Walker prospect	aquamarine, feldspar
Cabarrus	Concord, Harrisburg	chalcedony, opal
Caldwell		almandite, aquamarine
Catawba		almandite, citrine, emerald, rutilated

State and County	*Locality*	*Gemstone*
NORTH CAROLINA *(cont.)*		
Catawaba *(cont.)*		quartz, quartz crystal, rose quartz, smoky quartz
Clay	Cullakeene mine, Buck Creek	emerald, ruby matrix, corundum
	Shooting Creek	hyalite, opal, ruby, matrix, sapphire
Cleveland	Casar	rutilated quartz
	Kings Mountain	diamond
	Shelby, Hollybush prospect	emerald
	Turner mine	emerald
Davidson	Taro	amethyst
Franklin	Louisburg	amethyst
	Portis gold mine	diamond
Gaston		aquamarine, lazolite
Granville		jasper, amethyst
Haywood		amethyst
	Waynesville	green tourmaline
Henderson	Zirconia	zircon
Iredell		amethyst, opal, rose quartz, rutilated quartz
	Statesville	sunstone, amethyst
Jackson		almandite, rutilated quartz
	Grimshawes mine, Montvale	gem corundum, aquamarine
	Mason Branch Valley, near Franklin	rhodolite
	R. E. Brown prospect	aquamarine
	Sapphire and White Water mine	sapphire
Lincoln	Cottage Home	diamond
	Denver	amethyst
	Iron Station	amethyst
	Lincolnton	amethyst
McDowell		pyrope
	Dysortville, headwaters of Muddy Creek	diamond
Macon	Corundum Hill mine, Cullasaja	hyalite opal, emerald, sapphire
	Ellijay mine, Ellijay Creek	gem corundum
	Franklin area, Cowee Valley	ruby, rhodolite, amethyst, garnet (rhodolite)
	Littlefield mine, Tessentee Creek	amethyst, aquamarine, golden beryl
	Tremont Mountain	chrysoprase
Madison		opal
	Reeds Creek	aquamarine, jasper
Mecklenburg	Caldwell	chalcedony
	Todd's Branch	diamond

State and County	*Locality*	*Gemstone*
NORTH CAROLINA *(cont.)*		
Mitchell		almandite
	Bakersville area	aquamarine, emerald, essonite, quartz crystal, oligoclase
	Hawk mine	moonstone
	Crabtree Mountain, Emerald Matrix mine	emerald
	Medlock Mountain, Bakersville	sunstone
	Spruce Pine	emerald, corundum, garnet, golden beryl, zircon, moonstone, sunstone, kunzite
	Machone Mines	amazonite, spodumene
	Wiseman mine	aquamarine, emerald
Moore	Shut-in-Creek	jasper
Orange		chalcedony
Person		jasper
Randolph		rutilated quartz
Rowan	Gold Hill	sunstone
Rutherford	J.B. Twitty gold placer mine	diamond
Stokes	Dan River	rose quartz
Surry	Elkin and White Plains	quartz crystal
Transylvania		sapphire, quartz
Vance	Henderson	garnet
Warren	Inez, Warrenton	quartz, amethyst
Yancey		almandite
	Burnsville, Ray Mica mine	amazonite, aquamarine
NORTH DAKOTA		
Billings	Medora	wood
La Moure	Edgeley	garnet, iolite
McKenzie	Watford City	moss agate
Morton	Mandan	wood
Stark	Richardton	chalcedony
Williams	Williston	moss agate
OHIO		
Clermont	Milford	diamond
Muskingum	Zanesville	flint, opal
OKLAHOMA		
Comanche	Wichita Mountains	rutilated quartz

State and County	Locality	Gemstone
OKLAHOMA *(cont.)*		
McCurtain	Glover Creek	quartz crystal
Woods	Alva	wood, jasper, agate
	Tillman	wood, jasper, agate
	Beckham	wood, jasper, agate
OREGON		
Baker		malachite, precious opal, rhodolite, almandite
	Durkee	agate, jasper, opal
Benton	Willamette River	heliotrope, iris agate, jasper
Clatsop	Nehalem River	carnelian
Columbia	Vernonia	carnelian
Coos	Rock Creek	azurite, chrysocolla
Crook	Crooked River, Post	jasper, agate
	Carey Ranch	plume agate
	John Davis River	opal
	Eagle Rock	plume agate
	Ochoco	agate, plume agate, opal, jasper
Curry	Trinity River	diamond
Deschutes	Bend area	agate nodules
Douglas	Cedar Springs Mountain	azurite, malachite
	Nickel Mountain	chrysoprase
	bars on Umpqua River	grossularite, agate, jasper, carnelian
	Days Creek	jasper
	Central Point	agate
	Eagle Point	agate
	Butte Creek, Big Butte	agate, jasper
Harney		sapphire, wood, opal
Jackson	Camp White	amethyst, rhodonite, jasper, sagenite
Jefferson	Ashwood	opal, amethyst
	Priddy Ranch	thunder egg, "plume agate"
Josephine	Waldo and Galice districts	azurite, chrysocolla, malachite
	Cave Creek district	rhodonite
Lake	Lakeview	sanidine sunstone
	Glass Buttes	obsidian
	Hart Mountain	agate, jasper, geodes, opal
Lincoln	Newport Beach	heliotrope, wood
	Toledo	agate
	Salmon River and Cedar Creek, near Toledo	carnelian
Malheur		chalcedony, opal, wood

State and County	*Locality*	*Gemstone*
OREGON *(cont.)*		
Morrow	Opal Butte	opal, thunder eggs
Union	Starkey	agate
Wallowa	Joseph, on Lower Inmaha River	prase
Wasco	Antelope	iris agate, jasper, quartz
	Hood River	heliotrope
	Warm Springs Indian Reservation	agate
	Mosier	wood
PENNSYLVANIA		
Bedford	Bedford	amethyst, rock crystal
Berks	Fritz Island, near Reading	azurite, malachite, jasper
Bucks	Feasterville	sunstone
	Creeks Creek	almandine
	Neshaminy Creek	wood
	Pierce's Paper Mill	sunstone, labradorite
	Vanarts Dalen quarry	moonstone
Carbon	Hauto	quartz crystal
	Jim Thorpe	jasper
Chester		almandite, chrysoprase, jasper, moonstone, tourmaline
	Birmingham Township	amethyst
	Osburn Hill	quartz
	London Grove	quartz
	Chester	gem beryl
	East Bradford Township	amethyst
	French Creek	malachite
	Northrup	gem beryl
	Nottingham Township	sunstone
	Phoenixville	azurite
	Pocopson Township	amethyst
	Sadsbury Township	amethyst
	Unionville	jasper, moonstone
	Valley Township	amethyst, quartz
	Cumberland	wood, agate
Delaware		jasper, moonstone
	Avondale, Leiper quarry	almandite, aquamarine, essonite, green beryl
	Deshong's quarry	aquamarine, golden beryl
	Mineral Hill	amazonite
	Aston Township	amethyst
	Shaw and Esrey quarry	amethyst
	Linwood	beryl
	Brandywine	copper minerals
	Summit Howard House	rutilated quartz
	Leiperville	beryl, garnet, aquamarine
	Henry's quarry	amethyst

State and County	*Locality*	*Gemstone*
PENNSYLVANIA *(cont.)*		
Delaware *(cont.)*	Media	amazonite, amethyst, beryl
	Chichester Township	quartz, amethyst
	Chester Creek	amethyst, beryl, quartz
	Middletown Township	amazonite, amethyst
Huntingdon	Birmingham	amethyst
Lancaster		jasper, rutilated quartz, uvarovite, amethyst
	Rock Springs	carnelian, moss agate
	Wood's Chromite mine	uvarovite
Lebanon	Cornwall	azurite, malachite
Lehigh		andradite, malachite
Luzerne	White Haven	quartz crystals
Monroe	Stroudsburg	quartz crystal
Montgomery	Audubon	azurite, smoky quartz
	Perkiomen mine	azurite, malachite
	Philadelphia area	aquamarine
	Sumneytown	azurite
Northampton	Durham	jasper, chalcedony
	Bethlehem	jasper, prase
	South Mountain	catseye, quartz, chalcedony, prase
Perry	Millerstown	malachite
Philadelphia		smoky quartz, spessartite
	Falls of Schuylkill	amethyst
	Fairmount Park	beryl, spessartite
	Germantown	beryl, spessartite
	Logan	beryl, spessartite
	Mount Airy	beryl, spessartite
	Shawmont	beryl, spessartite
York	York Haven	wood
RHODE ISLAND		
Bristol	Portsmouth Ferry	quartz, amethystine
	Mt. Hope	agate
Kent	East Greenwich	agate, jasper, quartz
Lancaster	Texas	serpentine, williamsite
Providence	Calumet Hill quarry	jasper, rutilated quartz
	Centredale	quartz crystals
	Cumberland	agate, amethyst, smoky quartz
SOUTH CAROLINA		
Abbeville		amethyst
Anderson	Anderson, J.N.S. McConnell	aquamarine, green beryl, amethyst,

State and County	*Locality*	*Gemstone*
SOUTH CAROLINA *(cont.)*		
Anderson *(cont.)*		
	property Pelzer	sapphire, garnet
Cherokee	Rowen River	emerald, sapphire, garnet
Chesterfield	Brewer Mine	topaz
Greenwood	Callison	fire opal
	Shoals Junction	amethyst
Laurens	Waterloo	corundum
Richland	Columbia	amethyst
	Hells Canyon	agate
Union	Jonesville	amethyst
SOUTH DAKOTA		
Corson	Little Eagle	fairborn agate, rose quartz
	Elephant Gulch	pyrope, almandite
	Harney Peak	rose quartz
	Lawrence Whitewood	geodes with amethyst
Custer	Black Hills district	azurite, aquamarine, golden beryl, hiddenite, petrified wood, rose quartz, tourmaline
	Scott quarry	opal
	Scott Rose quartz mine, Custer	rose quartz
Meade	Fox Ridge	wood, agate
Minnehaha	Sioux Falls	jasper
Pennington	Black Hills district	azurite, aquamarine, golden beryl, hiddenite, petrified wood, rose quartz, tourmaline
	Imlay	geodes
	Keystone	beryl, tourmaline
	Scenic	fairborn agate
TENNESSEE		
Hamblen	Russellville	quartz crystal
Monroe		malachite
	Koko Creek, Tellico River	diamond
Polk	Ducktown	azurite, malachite
Roane	Clinch River, near Union Crossroads	diamond
Union	Luttrell, Flat Creek	diamond
TEXAS		
Anderson	Palestine	topaz

State and County	*Locality*	*Gemstone*
TEXAS *(cont.)*		
Armstrong	Paloduro Canyon	wood
Bastrop		wood
Bexar	San Antonio, Reese River	prase
Brewster	Marfa-Alpine	agate
	Byrd Ranch Alpine	labradorite
	Haley Peak	fire opal
	Woodward Ranch	opal, agate (Texas plume)
Burnet		amethyst
Colorado		wood
Culberson	Van Horn	turquoise
El Paso		amethyst
Fayette		quartz crystal, wood
Gonzales		wood
Jeff Davis	Fort Davis	jasper
Hildago	Sullivan City	jasper
Hudspeth		carnelian
Llano	Llano	agate, amethyst, opal, rose quartz, topaz, quartz (ilanite)
	Grit	topaz
Mason	Katemcy	amazonite, topaz
	Streeter	topaz
Parker	Silver Peak	prase
Presidio	Shafter	chrysocolla, malachite
	Rogel Ranch	agate
San Patricio		agate
Starr	Rio Grande River	agate
Uvalde	Montell Freer	wood
Walker	Huntsville	diamond
Webb	Laredo	agate, jasper, wood
Zapata		agate, jasper, wood
UTAH		
Beaver		azurite, malachite, agate
	Copper Gulch, Starr and Frisco districts	garnet
	Newfoundland	malachite

State and County	*Locality*	*Gemstone*
UTAH *(cont.)*		
Beaver *(cont.)*	Promontory Point	malachite
	Sierra Madre	malachite
	Mineral Mountains	smoky quartz
Cache	La Plata	azurite, malachite
Davis	Farmington mine	azurite, malachite
	Wandering Jew mine	azurite, malachite
Emery	Castle Valley district	azurite, malachite
	San Rafael Swell	wood, agate, jasper
Garfield	Circle Cliffs	wood
Grand		azurite, agate
	Agate Switch	agate
Iron	Gold Springs	garnet
Juab	Thomas Mountains	garnet, topaz
	Tintic	azurite, chrysocolla
	Jehicho	agate
	Levan	agate
Millard	Clear Lake	labradorite
Morgan	Copper Mountain mine	azurite, malachite
Piute	Deer Creek	garnet
	Ohio district	malachite
Salt Lake	Big and Little Cottonwood	azurite, garnet, malachite
	Old Jordan mine, Bingham	opal
	Bingham Canyon	azurite, malachite
San Juan	Navajo Reservation	pyrope, spessartite
	La Sal district	azurite, malachite
Sevier	Ball mine	wood
	Sevier Canyon	wood
Tooele	Clifton	azurite, garnet, malachite
	Drum Mountain	jasper, agate
	Dugway	amethyst
	Ibapah Mountains	aquamarine
	Amatrice Mine	variscite
	Simpson Springs	morganite
Uintah	Dyer Mine	azurite, malachite
Utah	American Fork	garnet
	Fairfield	variscite
	Goshen	agate
Washington	Dixie and Silver Reef	azurite
	Lucern Claim	garnet, malachite
Wayne	Hanksville	wood, agate

State and County	*Locality*	*Gemstone*
UTAH *(cont.)*		
Weber	New Azurite mine	azurite, malachite
	Ogden Boilermaker mine	azurite, malachite
	Strong's Canyon	garnet
	Golden	topaz
VERMONT		
Orange	Copper mines at Corinth, Copperfield and South Strafford	malachite
	Topsham	rhodonite
Rutland	West Hartford	rutilated quartz
	Ira	chrysocolla
Washington	Waterbury	rutilated quartz, staurolite
	Cabot	rutilated quartz, staurolite
Windsor	South Royalton	quartz crystal
VIRGINIA		
Amelia	Amelia Court House	amazonite, beryl, amethyst, rutilated quartz, spessartite
	Champion Mine	moonstone
	Morefield Mine	topaz, amazonite
	Richeson Mica Mine	amazonite
	Rutherford Mine	topaz, amazonite, spessartite
Amherst		rutilated quartz
	Fanch Hill	amethyst
	Lowesville	amethyst
Campbell		turquoise crystals
	Brookneal	amethyst
Charlotte	Charlotte Court House	amethyst
Chesterfield	Manchester	diamond
Fairfax	Fairfax	gem quartz
Goochland	O.W. Harris Mica Mine Farm	moonstone
Hanover	Hewlett	moonstone, sunstone
Henry	Axton	staurolite, beryl
Louisa	Trevilians	amethyst
Madison	Fisher's Gap	azurite
Mecklenburg	Pontiac mine	azurite
Nelson		amethyst
Page	Luray	azurite
	Ida	jasper, hematite, epidite

State and County	*Locality*	*Gemstone*
VIRGINIA *(cont.)*		
Patrick		staurolite, beryl
Prince Edward	Rice	amethyst, quartz
Prince William	Minnieville	amethyst
Rockbridge	Irish Creek	beryl
Rockingham	High Knob Elkton	azurite
Warren	Bentonville	azurite
	Front Royal	azurite, chrysocolla
WASHINGTON		
Benton		blue agate, amethyst, opal, wood
Chelan	Crown Point mine	quartz crystal
Clark	Bell Mountain mine	gem quartz
Cowlitz	Cloverdale	agate, carnelian, amethyst
Ferry	Republic mining district	gold
Grant	Corfu	wood
	Smyrna Vantage	agate
Jefferson	Mound Anderson	gem quartz
	Agate Bench	agate
	Rustler Creek	gem quartz
King	Denny Mountain	gem quartz
Kittitas		jasper, opal, wood, blue agate, amethyst
Klickitat	Horse Heaven Hills	opalized wood, wood
	Warwick	agate, carnelian, jasper, wood
Lewis		carnelian, agate, jasper, wood, opal
	Chehalis River	carnelian
Lincoln	Davenport	precious opal
Okanogan	Okanogan	agate
Pend Oreille	Newport	amethyst
Pierce	Old Siegmund Ranch	amethystine quartz
Skagit	Sedro Woolley	nephrite
Skamania	Rainbow	amethyst
Snohomish	Monte Cristo district	malachite
	Vesper Peak	essonite
Walla Walla	Whitman Creek	opal
Whitman	Whelan locality near Pullman	precious opal
	Moses locality, Clarkston	precious opal

State and County	Locality	Gemstone
WEST VIRGINIA		
Monroe	Peterstown	diamond
WISCONSIN		
Dane	Oregon	feldspar
Marathon	Moonstone	feldspar
	Wausau	albite peristerite
Ozaukee	Saukville	feldspar
Pierce	Plum Creek	feldspar
Racine	Burlington	feldspar
St. Croix	Lake St. Croix	agate
Washington	Kohlsville	feldspar
Waukesha	Eagle	feldspar
Wood	Wisconsin Rapids	rose quartz
WYOMING		
Albany	Holmes, Grand Encampment district	azurite, malachite
Big Horn	Crazy Woman Petrified Forest	wood
Carbon	Sweetwater River	moss agate, jade, malachite
	Encampment	amethyst
Converse	Boxelder Creek	geodes
Crook	Warren's Peak	azurite
Fremont	Lander	nephrite, corundum
	Long Creek	moss agate, jade
	Marion Claim	ruby
	Sage Hen Creek	moss agate
	Townships 30, 31, Ranges 89, 90, 91	agate
	Wind River	agate
	Riverton	moss agate
Goshen		azurite, garnet, chrysocolla, malachite
Johnson	Bighorn Mountains	azurite
Laramie	Chugwater	heliotrope
Natrona	Sage Hen Creek	moss agate
Park	Kirwin	malachite
Platte	Wilde and Deercorn mine	moss agate
	Guernsey	moss agate
	Hartville	moss agate

State and County	*Locality*	*Gemstone*
WYOMING *(cont.)*		
Sweetwater	Eden Valley	petrified wood
	Yellowstone National Park	amethyst, agate, petrified wood, agate
	Eden Valley	wood
	Bairoil	wood
	Farson	wood
Uinta	Green River to Fort Bridger	wood, jasper, quartz
Yellowstone Park (no collecting)	Amethyst Mountain	fossil forests

Selected Bibliography

Dana, Edward S., *A Textbook of Mineralogy.* New York: John Wiley and Sons, 1958.

Desautels, Paul E., *The Gem Kingdom.* New York: Random House, Inc. 1970.

Hayes, George Gibbons, *Where to Prospect in the 50 States.* Nugget Publishing Co., 1964.

Kunz, George F., *Gems and Precious Stones of North America.* New York: Dover Publishing Company, 1968.

MacFall, Russell P., *Gem Hunter's Guide,* 2nd ed. Chicago: Science and Mechanics Company, 1958.

Pearl, Richard M., *Colorado Gem Trails and Mineral Guide.* Denver, Colo.: Sage Books, 1958.

Pearl, Richard M., *How to Know the Minerals and Rocks.* New York: McGraw-Hill Publishing Company, 1955.

Pough, Frederick H., *A Field Guide to Rocks and Minerals.* San Diego: Lapidary Journal Book Department, 3rd edition.

Quick, Lelande, *The Book of Agates.* Philadelphia: Chilton Book Co., 1970.

Schlegel, Dorothy M., *Gemstones of the United States.* Washington, D.C.: United States Department of the Interior, Superintendent of Documents, Geological Survey Bulletin 1042-G, 1957.

Simpson, Bessie W., *Gem Trails of Arizona.* Glen Rose, Texas: Gem Trails Publishing Co., 1970.

Sinkankas, John, *Gemstones of North America.* Princeton, N.J.: D. Van Nostrand Company, 1959.

Sinkankas, John, *Prospecting for Gems and Minerals.* New York: D. Van Nostrand Company, 1970.

Sinkankas, John, *Gem Cutting.* New York: Random House, Inc. 1970.

Sperisen, Francis J., *The Art of Lapidary.* New York: Bruce Publishing Company, 1961.

Strong, Mary F., ed., *Desert Gem Trails,* 2nd rev. ed. Mentone, Calif.: Gembooks, 1965.

Wald, Robert, *Jewelry Making as a Hobby.* New York: Association Press, 1972.

Zeitner, June C., *Appalachian Mineral and Gem Trails.* Mentone, Calif.: Gembooks.

Zeitner, June C., *Midwest Gem Trails Field Guide.* Mentone, Calif.: Gembooks.

Zeitner, June C., *Southwest Mineral and Gem Trails.* Mentone, Calif.: Gembooks.

Index